A
Woman's
Heart
That
Dances

A Woman's Heart That Dances

CATHERINE MARTIN

HARVEST HOUSE PUBLISHERS

EUGENE, OREGON

Cover by Koechel Peterson & Associates, Inc., Minneapolis, Minnesota

Cover illustration by Kathleen L. Rousar, used by permission copyright © 2009 Kathleen L. Rousar / www.klrousar.com

Published in association with the literary agency of WordServe Literary Group, Ltd., 10152 S. Knoll Circle, Highlands Ranch, CO 80130

Every effort has been made to give proper credit for all stories, poems, and quotations. If for any reason proper credit has not been given, please notify the author or publisher and proper notation will be given on future printing.

This book includes stories in which the author has changed people's names and some details of their situation in order to protect their privacy.

A WOMAN'S HEART THAT DANCES
Copyright © 2009 by Catherine Martin
Published by Harvest House Publishers
Eugene, Oregon 97402
www.harvesthousepublishers.com

Library of Congress Cataloging-in-Publication Data
Martin, Catherine
A woman's heart that dances / Catherine Martin.
    p. cm.
ISBN 978-0-7369-2640-9 (pbk.)
1. Christian women—Religious life. 2. Spirituality. 3. Dance—Religious aspects—Christianity.
I. Title.
BV4527.M267 2009
248.8'43—dc22
                                        2009004728

Printed in the United States of America
            09 10 11 12 13 14 15 16 17 / VP-SK / 10 9 8 7 6 5 4 3 2 1

To my father,
Robert Joseph Snyder,
on the occasion of his eightieth birthday.

Dad, you are one of God's great gifts to me,
and I'm so thankful for the love we've shared over the years.

Thank you for encouraging me to never give up,
to always pursue my dreams,
and to believe that nothing is impossible with God.

I love you.

Acknowledgments

First, thank You, Lord, for the dance and for painting beautiful color into all my days.

To my beloved husband, David, and to Mother and Dad, Rob, Tania, Kayla, Christopher, Eloise, Andy, Eloise, Keegan, and James: thank you for your love, patience, and encouragement.

Thank you to Kathleen Rousar for permission to print four of your beautiful ballerina paintings in this book. You have captured in a unique way what it means to be a dancer.

Thank you to Ney Bailey for teaching me to dance in my relationship with the Lord. I will forever be thankful to you for showing me how important the Word of God is in my faith. And thank you to Josh McDowell for showing me that the Bible is the authority for my belief.

Thank you to Jim Smoke for encouraging me to write. And thank you especially to Dottie McDowell, Andy Graybill, Leann McGee, and Vonette Bright for showing me how to dance with the Lord.

And thank you to all the dancers in my life—all you dear sisters in the Lord who encourage me by stepping into the embrace of Jesus, following His lead: my friends from the early days of Campus Crusade at Arizona State University and on staff with CCC, my fellow Bible study girls in San Diego, the women at SCC, my friends here in the desert and throughout the world. You have all helped me understand my own dance better and write about it here. A special thanks to Tom and Tracy Stickel for providing an amazing place to write about the dance.

Thank you to my special friends in publishing for helping bring this book to print and getting it into the hands of others throughout the world—Bob Hawkins Jr., Gene Skinner (my editor), and the entire team of Harvest House Publishers. Thank you to Greg Johnson, my agent at WordServe Literary.

Finally, thank you to the Quiet Time Ministries team, financial and prayer partners, and board of directors for serving alongside me as we continue together in our dance with the Lord.

Contents

There is…a time to dance.
ECCLESIASTES 3:4 NCV

David was dancing before the LORD with all his might…
I will celebrate before the LORD.
2 SAMUEL 6:14,21

You have turned my mourning into joyful dancing.
You have taken away my clothes of mourning
and clothed me with joy,
that I might sing praises to you and not be silent.
O LORD my God, I will give you thanks forever!
PSALM 30:11-12 NLT

Let them praise His name with dancing;
Let them sing praises to Him with timbrel and lyre.
For the LORD takes pleasure in His people;
He will beautify the afflicted ones with salvation.
PSALM 149:3-4

by Ney Bailey

I love this statement, which Catherine quotes in her book: "You be responsible for the depth of your ministry and let God be responsible for its breadth." Catherine Martin has certainly taken these words to heart. She has spent hours in God's presence probing the depths of His Word, and He has taught her well. In turn, she has been faithful to teach others—and now that teaching has multiplied around the world through her books and media.

Catherine's teaching is relevant, practical, biblical, and full of stories that draw us in and make the Word of God applicable personally. She is not only a gifted teacher but also a ballet dancer. In a unique way she invites us to recognize the Lord's initiation toward us, and she encourages us to allow Him to lead as we learn to dance with Him. As we choose to follow His lead, we inevitably fall in love with Him more and more each day.

I have never been much of a dancer on the outside, but this book encouraged me to dance on the inside in my own relationship with the Lord. Just as I have been, I believe you will be drawn into *A Woman's Heart That Dances* and will experience a closer, more intimate relationship with Jesus.

Ney Bailey

Introduction

Welcome to a love story—a story about your relationship with the Lord Jesus that uses the imagery of dance. This love story is for you and about you. For above all else, the Lord loves you with an everlasting love. Someday your prince will come, says the fairy tale. But the Bible assures us that our Prince has *already* come. He is Jesus, the Prince of Peace and the Prince of life. From nearly every chapter, intertwined in almost every verse throughout the Bible, over and over again, your Prince invites you to spectacular adventures and surprising journeys with Him. He invites you, *Will you dance with Me?* As we begin this love story, I pray that regardless of who you are or what circumstances you find yourself in, you may heartily respond to your blessed Prince's invitation and say a thousand times over, *Yes, Lord, I will dance with you.* Jesus promises your life will never be the same. He promises you abundant and eternal life. He promises.

In His love from another dancer,

Catherine

Part 1

Lord, I Will
Dance with You

Dance

Jenny was plain, not pretty like some other girls. Indeed, in front of the mirror, Jenny sometimes felt ugly, worthless, and unlovable. High school teens tend to be at least as shallow as adults, so kids at school made Jenny's life miserable. She went to all the school dances, but she was never asked to dance. The other girls teased her mercilessly, and the boys often raised her hopes only to let her down.

One night Jenny cried herself to sleep after attending a school dance. She had dressed up in her prettiest clothes, put on her makeup, and gone to the dance with high hopes. Someone would surely ask her to dance. But all through the dance she sat alone on a chair next to the wall. A couple of times her heart leaped when a boy came toward her, but then her heart sank when he asked one of the other girls to dance. Tears drenched her pillow that night. Anger, bitterness, and pain rocked her to sleep.

But then the remarkable happened. A restless, fitful sleep was suddenly transformed into a marvelous, fantastic dream. In her dream she was at a magnificent dance—the spectacular dance hall was filled to perfection with streamers and laughter and music. Silver balls hung from the ceiling, spraying bits of light that flashed over the entire gathering, bounced from the dance floor, spilled off the walls, and lit up faces. The handsome men were all dressed in tuxedos. The elegant women wore formal gowns of lace and silk and were adorned with orchid corsages. Jenny was dressed in her finest, standing alone next to the wall.

Suddenly the doors swung open, revealing the most handsome man she had ever seen. He was so beautiful that all the dancers stopped in midstep just to look at him. He made his way across the dance floor right to where Jenny was standing. With a smile on his face, he looked into her eyes, held out his hand, and said, "Jenny, will you dance with me?"

She was stunned—shocked to disbelief. She desperately searched faces in the crowd to determine whether this was a practical joke. Were they smirking? Laughing at her? She had been cruelly tricked like this before. But this beautiful man kept looking directly into her eyes and insisted, "Jenny, I'd like to dance with you." At that moment, with her heart on her sleeve, she trusted that he sincerely desired to dance with her. She would dance!

But Jenny didn't know how to dance. No one had ever asked her before. And even though she felt clumsy and awkward as the handsome stranger whisked her to the dance floor, she found herself safely in his arms. Soon she was dancing with abandon, thrilled to discover a divine freedom as she followed his lead. She floated on air without a care in the world, her soul overflowing with joy. She could dance!

"I've wanted to dance with you for a long time, Jenny," the handsome stranger said, drawing her close. She could hardly believe what she was hearing! Then she heard him say, "I love you, Jenny. I love you with all my heart and all my soul and all my strength." Cautiously, she searched his eyes. She could see the passion of his unconditional love. And suddenly she knew the name of this beautiful stranger. She was dancing with Jesus.

Jenny is every girl in her most awkward and difficult moments. We have all experienced those times when we think, *No one likes me. No one even knows I exist. I don't see any hope for my life.* You can replace her name with your name. Or you can fill in a friend's name. Or add mine, for that matter. The astounding truth is that whoever you are, whatever you have done, and however impossible your circumstances may be, Jesus, who loves to dance, wants to dance with you.

She was alone in the world and was nothing much to look at. Her husband had died and left her with no real resources. Rising from the table, she put on her shawl and walked over to the place where she kept her money. She had watched her small savings dwindle down to two copper coins. She was no one of importance to those in her world, but her heart was well-known to the One who mattered most of all. She was a great heart to heaven's watching eyes—confident, trusting in God's provision, and surrendered. Her hands gripped her last two coins, knowing once her money was gone, her needs would still be met somehow, in some way, by the God of all creation. And so she walked up the steps of the temple, past the porticoes, into the Court of Women. Making her way to the temple box, she gave her gift to God.

Few people noticed her, but Someone was watching. And He esteemed her in the presence of all who were with Him. Why? Because she was a dancer. "I tell you the truth," Jesus said, "this poor widow has put in more than all the others. All these people gave their gifts out of their wealth; but she out of her poverty put in all she had to live on" (Luke 21:3-4). On that momentous day, a poor widow sacrificed all she had, displaying to the watching world her trust in God. She was dancing, fully surrendered in the embrace of the One who had created her. Jesus wanted His disciples to know how to dance in a difficult world. And perhaps, at that moment, He smiled, knowing He and a poor widow who understood life's greatest secret would continue to dance into eternity.

Jesus dances with imperfect people on stages of poverty and brokenness, abundance and joy. He is not who we think He is. He is more—so much more. He sees clear to the heart. He shows up when no one else does. He loves unabashedly, almost shocking a heart with the wealth of His compassion and kindness. Always, always He is looking into the eyes of your heart, inviting you to His blessed, assuring embrace, ready to lead you in a dance uniquely designed just for you and Him.

Nicole walked into a room filled with 400 worshipping women. In her self-confident days, she would have felt no fear. But now, uneasiness washed over her, a by-product of the troubles of recent years. Once she had been on top of her world, a graduate of a highly accredited university and a professional athlete. Now she was homeless, jobless, and alone. *How could someone like me be in so much trouble?* she may have thought in her sorrow.

But things were different now that she had made a decision. She had surrendered her life to Jesus. She wanted to know Him more. Bravely, she walked into the room and prayed, *Lord, show me where to sit.* Her eyes were drawn to an empty seat next to another young woman, so she made her way there as the worship team led a song of surrender. She had never met the woman next to her, but she felt drawn to her as she watched her worship the Lord on her knees with one hand extended to heaven. As Nicole listened to the song and watched this woman, she sensed something she had not known before—a love and power penetrating her own heart and soul. The worship team closed in prayer, but Nicole couldn't move or pull her eyes from the woman sitting next to her.

The woman said to Nicole, "Welcome to Bible study. May I hug you?"

Tears threatened to fill Nicole's eyes. "Yes. I'm new here. I don't know anyone."

"Well, my name is Veronica. I'm a leader in one of the Bible studies. Why don't you join my group?"

I met Nicole a week later when Veronica introduced me to her, "Catherine, we have to tell you the story of what God has done!" As

Nicole excitedly shared how the Lord had directed her to sit next to Veronica, tears filled my eyes too. I thought, *It's the dance. It's all about the dance. Jesus is dancing an amazing, beautiful, spectacular dance with my precious sisters. Only He could work together so many steps into such a story.* Nicole's intelligent eyes were filled with hope, and I was suddenly overwhelmed with the realization that Jesus had asked her to dance.

Words tumbled from my lips. "Nicole, you are so very special to Jesus. You mean everything to Him. He has reached through the heavens to invite you to dance. And you have leaned into His embrace with all your heart. From now on, you can trust Him to lead you. That's why your dance with Him will be such a great adventure. He knows you better than you know yourself, for He created you. He knows your brilliance, your giftedness. And you need to know the great respect He has for you as a woman. He clearly esteemed women in His day, and He wants you to know how important you are to Him. Your adventure with the Lord will be filled with hills and valleys, difficult times and joyful times, but the view will be breathtaking. And now, Nicole, get ready to dance with Him. Oh, how you will dance."

How could I make such claims to a young woman who was facing uncertain times? I myself have known the importance of the dance in my own adversities. Jesus has led me onto unique stages, custom-designed just for me, when I could find no way out of my troubles. And in the course of our dance together, Jesus has taken me to the experience of a new day, when I caught a glimpse of His plans and purposes.

I first learned about the dance from David, the shepherd boy who became king of Israel. At first, the idea of the dance surprised me. And the more I've grown in my understanding of the dance, the more it has astonished me. I will never be the same because of the dance. The same can be true for you.

Early in my dance with the Lord, I had heard others say David was a man after God's heart. Becoming a woman after God's heart sounded like a worthwhile goal to me. But understanding the heart of David became much more important when I finally read about him firsthand in the Bible. I learned that God Himself said, "I have found David the son of Jesse, a man after My heart" (Acts 13:22; see also 1 Samuel 13:14). Now, that's impressive as far as I'm concerned. It's one thing if my best friend says, "Catherine, you are a woman after God's heart." But it's quite another if God proclaims joyfully to others, "Catherine is a woman after My heart." Wow! *That* calls for a real celebration.

When God spoke of David in such glowing terms, He added, "David...will do all my will." God was saying that David responded to His leading, moving in synergy with His desires. And God was further saying He loved David's willingness and responsiveness. David pleased Him. God led, and David followed. When David brought the ark of the covenant to Jerusalem, he celebrated and danced before the Lord with all his might (2 Samuel 6:14). He was dancing *with* the Lord, and not just outwardly, but from the heart.

How do I know David also danced inwardly, from the heart? God declares that He doesn't look at outward appearances—He looks at the heart (1 Samuel 16:7). He is always looking for hearts that are especially surrendered to Him and completely His (2 Chronicles 16:9). And there was David, just such a person, ready to move with God in total and even reckless abandonment to Him. David's heart danced with the Lord. And because David danced with Him, God accomplished great and mighty works in and through his life.

Dancing is a metaphor that helps us understand the practicalities and possibilities of our relationship with God. Metaphors are designed to take our imaginations in new directions. Metaphorical language, according to one author, is "like gum...to be chewed over and savored, not gulped down!"[1] Another author describes metaphor as "a kind of magical mental changing room—where one thing, for a moment, becomes another, and in that moment is seen in a whole new way...As soon as something old is seen in a new way, it stimulates a torrent of new thoughts and associations, almost as if a mental floodgate has been lifted."[2]

The imagery of the dance begins with the overture or invitation to dance. Then comes a response, when one says yes to another. The dance itself begins, and a partnership is formed. As we dance with the Lord, the realization gradually dawns on us—*I am a dancer, and I love the One with whom I am dancing*. The dancer surrenders, leans in to the embrace of her partner, and allows him to take the lead. As she focuses on him and responds to him, romance and intimacy characterize the relationship. She learns new steps, sometimes surprising ones, and each move beautifully expresses their story to the world. And the greatest dance of all, your dance with the Lord, never ends—it lasts forever.

Thinking deeply and devotionally about the dance will enrich your relationship with God in ways you can appreciate only when you are actually living out the dance itself. Just imagine the wonder of discovering that the Lord is inviting you, like Jenny, to draw near to Him, surrender to His leading, and dance with Him every moment of your life. You will be moving in response to His guidance. The applications are endless when you think of your life with God as a dance. The writer of Ecclesiastes understood this blessed metaphor when he declared, "There is a time...to dance" (Ecclesiastes 3:4 NCV). For you, the time to dance is now.

One of the greatest dancing partnerships on film was the duo of Fred Astaire and Eleanor Powell. I recently saw a video clip of Astaire and Powell dancing to Cole Porter's Broadway melody "Begin the Beguine." Astaire is clearly leading, but Powell is so experienced in the dance that her feet move in perfect timing with his steps. Astaire adds new steps with each stanza of the music, leading in entirely new directions. But Powell is so focused on him that when he moves, she is able to follow with virtually no lag time between his steps and hers. And so they dance in perfect harmony while the audience watches with awe and amazement. So it is with us. You can always spot people who are comfortable dancing with the Lord, for they move with design and precision, led by their unseen yet very real eternal dance Partner. When we dance with the Lord, the world looks on with wonder and amazement. A dancer stands out in a world of people sitting alone along the wall.

I think of a beautiful prima ballerina, the tulle of her flowing dress moving gracefully as she dances on pointe across the stage. She creates the illusion of effortlessly floating on air. Imagine yourself dancing with Jesus and enjoying the fulfillment of His promise of rest for your soul. This dance is real! He extends his hand to you and asks you to join Him, to experience His beauty and feel the embrace of His love as you follow His lead in a life you've only dreamed of.

Our hearts and souls require the dance. We run through our days at such breakneck speed that we become blind to the true meaning of life. We get burned and battered on the inside with the multitude of details and distractions that our culture throws our way. We need relief and refreshment from the busyness and stress in our lives. We need rest for our souls. And Jesus is just the One to give it to us, for He is the lover of our souls. He promises the very rest we need when we come to Him and dance (Matthew 11:28-30). Rest is always available for those who live in the shelter of the Most High God and abide in the shadow of the Almighty (Psalm 91:1).

Where have we gone wrong? Why have we lost the reality of this beautiful dance with the Lord? In the 1960s, a new word invaded our vocabulary—*multitasking*. Multitasking has become an absolute norm for most people. One man describes his adventure driving on a busy freeway. He looks to his left and sees a young woman driving in the fast lane. "It was the first time I had seen anyone eating breakfast, talking on the phone, putting on her makeup, and sorting through papers while driving 65 miles an hour." If that weren't enough, the driver just behind her was reading a newspaper, drinking coffee, and yelling at the kids in the backseat.

One woman read an article listing the typical symptoms of stress—eating too much, buying impulsively, and driving too fast. She responded, "Are you kidding? That's my idea of a perfect day!" None of us is immune to the busyness of life. At one time I carried in my purse a Palm Treo, a BlackBerry, an iPhone, two Bluetooth headsets, a digital camera, and a wireless Internet access card. Thankfully, I've pared down my technological nightmare.

But I am still busy working 40 hours a week, writing books, and speaking throughout the United States. I'm still a wife, an aunt, a sister, and a daughter. And I still need to stay connected to e-mail and the telephone. I would venture to say your life is busy as well. And busyness can lead to stress, and stress can lead to burnout. Maybe you can relate to the person who said, "Just when I was getting used to yesterday, along came today." Or maybe you need the message one person read on her screen: "You've been online for one year—do you wish to log off and get a life?"

I have always loved the children's book *Alexander and the Terrible, Horrible, No Good, Very Bad Day*. Everything is always against him—like the time everyone got a donut in their lunchbox except Alexander. Or when he had to go to the dentist while everyone else played. Or when his teacher liked everyone's drawing except his own of the invisible castle. Alexander decided that he must move far away to Australia to get away from the terrible, horrible, no good, very bad day.

But perhaps you have already discovered, like me, that in life we rarely have the option of switching channels. We wish we had a remote control and could simply change to something new. Perhaps we are hoping to escape our difficulties by moving to Australia, just like Alexander. But usually, we're not afforded such a luxury.

Maybe you feel like Chippie, the parakeet described by Max Lucado. Chippie's disastrous day began when his owner decided to clean his cage with a vacuum cleaner. The phone rang, and she turned for a split second to answer it. When she turned back around, Chippie had vanished. Panic-stricken, she tore open the vacuum bag, and there was Chippie, covered in dust, coughing uncontrollably, and gulping in huge breaths of air. She carried him to the bathroom and held him under the faucet to clean him off. Then, realizing that Chippie was now completely drenched and shivering from the cold, she reached for the hair dryer! Well, Chippie was never the same. His owner remarked, "Chippie doesn't sing much anymore. He just sits and stares."

Have you ever felt like Chippie? One minute you're breezing along in life, and the next minute you wonder what hit you—your life has become overwhelming. I've felt that way. On some days, if it could go wrong, it did. Like the day my husband and I moved into a new desert home in 120-degree heat. The moving van was too heavy for the driveway, so we had to shuttle boxes from the van down a long driveway in the stifling heat to our house! Or the day I was in a hurry to a speaking engagement and got a flat tire right in the middle of a busy expressway. Or the day I was getting ready to speak and spilled coffee all over my clothes. Or the day I was late to work and road construction blocked my path all along the way. After a while, life's adversities can begin to wear you down. You know how it is—you're running through life at breakneck speed, you finally arrive at your destination, and the first person you see asks you how you are.

"Fine. How about you?"

"Fine."

And you know what *fine* means: Freaked-out, Insecure, Neurotic, and Emotional. We are on a treadmill, and someone is revving up the speed and increasing the incline. We are going faster and more furiously than ever before, and…and…wait a minute! Let's stop! Step off the treadmill, take a deep breath, and look at the One who is holding His hand out to you. Leave the treadmill behind and engage in the dance. For when we truly dance, keeping in step with the Lord and moving with Him at His pace, we will find what we long for— renewal, refreshment, and rest for our souls.

We dance with the Lord not only in the good times but even in impossible situations. He wants to lead us in the dance through all aspects of our lives. I discovered a faulty pattern in my thinking about life a number of years ago, and the Lord used the metaphor of the dance to help me discover this error.

When my mother was in an accident and broke her neck some years ago, I earnestly sought to escape from the traumatic experience rather than embrace it. And who wouldn't feel that way? Indeed, I prayed for God to heal her. And, in fact, her broken neck did heal, and she was not paralyzed. But throughout the next year, with every new difficulty that arose from my mother's trauma, I endeavored to get her out of the situation and into a better, happier circumstance. I became incredibly frustrated and brokenhearted when I realized I could not change the devastating results of my mother's multiple sclerosis, which precipitated the break. I became overwhelmingly depressed and sometimes wanted to give up entirely. I felt like lying down and not going on. I wasn't certain how anyone could give up on the responsibilities of life, but I was ready to find out.

One day in the midst of my crisis, my thoughts turned to the dance. I thought about the Lord's gracious and constant invitation to us to join Him. Then I thought of David's words in Psalm 30:11: "You have turned for me my mourning into dancing; You have loosed my sackcloth and girded me with gladness." In an instant, my mind went to a new place, and I spoke to the Lord out loud: "Lord, You want to dance with me, even in this terrible situation, don't You!" Instead of fleeing my difficulty so I could once again dance with the Lord, I realized that I could dance with Him *in* my trouble. The metaphor of the dance helped me draw near to the Lord, lean in to His blessed embrace, and allow Him to lead me through a most painful and emotional experience.

I realized that I was separating the circumstances of my life into two groups—those events that seemed to be going well and those that weren't going so great. I savored the good times and wanted to rid myself of the bad times. I tried to turn every difficulty into something better. Now, don't get me wrong—nothing is wrong with praying in the midst of our adversity for God to rescue us. But deep down, I had believed that God was blessing me when times were good and not when times were bad. When my life was a disaster, I thought I had lost God's favor. I needed to get out of the bad circumstances and into a stress-free life, where I felt God would once again be able to carry out His plan for me. It never occurred to me that perhaps God could weave the dark threads of my painful experiences into the fabric of my life and create something new and unexpected and beautiful. I had never imagined that the Lord leads us even in the valleys, where the sun never seems to shine. I never realized the special blessing of dancing with Him in the darkness.

We can dance with the Lord through every aspect of our lives. In every situation—easy or hard, good or bad, simple or difficult—the Lord wants to dance with you. Our Lord is extending His hand to you, inviting you to lean in to His embrace. As you respond to Him and follow His lead, He can fulfill His plan for your life and empower you to accomplish the wonderful things He is calling you to do. The secret to the dance lies in the answers to questions like these: How can we step closer to the Lord and follow His lead? Specifically, how can we dance in the midst of sorrow and pain? How can we dance if our husband has informed us that he is leaving? How can we dance if our child is an alcoholic? How can we dance if our mother or father has just died? How in the world can we surrender to His lead?

My friend, when you and I say yes to the Lord's invitation to dance, we will no longer merely trudge along in desperate aimlessness. Instead, we will begin an adventure of love, intimacy, and yes, even excitement. When we dance with the Lord, we are never alone in our circumstance, whatever it may be. We enjoy intimacy with the most beautiful, amazing, and powerful person we will ever meet, the Lord Jesus Christ. In our intimacy with Him, we experience an exchange of love, conversation, and communion through His Word and the indwelling Holy Spirit. This experience of intimacy with Jesus is not meant to be an unrealistic or faraway ideal; we can enjoy it in the midst of our everyday lives.

When we dance with Him, we no longer control our own lives. We relinquish, gladly and happily, the lead to the One who knows what He is doing. He loves us completely, He thinks we are beautiful, and He can accomplish anything in every impossible situation. Learning to dance with Jesus helps us understand the real and true context for every circumstance of our lives, including both the joys and the disappointments. The dance is beautiful, and it is powerful. We need not resign ourselves to meaningless hours and days. We can be actively engaged in purpose-filled moments that our eternal dance Partner meticulously designs.

I have experienced the power of the dance. My life has not been easy. In fact, I have experienced many losses with my loved ones, homes, professions, health, and more. I've experienced disappointments, and I live with unrealized dreams. I've often felt insignificant and invisible. Life has seemed impossible for me at times, and I've been tempted to give up. I'm thankful for the tough days for at least one reason—I've often said that you cannot write about experiences you've never had. I do know what it is to struggle with anxiety, fear, insecurity, bitterness, and resentment. You might not know that from looking at me because I often have a smile on my face. Joy is not the absence of suffering, but the presence of God. I've learned to dance with the Lord in the deepest and darkest of times.

My husband said, "Catherine, when you write this book, you are going to be the one to talk about how to dance when times are tough." And that is the secret I want to share with you. I want you to know the great hope in the dance—the very presence of the Lord Himself, regardless of what you face today or tomorrow. The Lord is always with you, and He is always extending His hand and saying, "Let's dance. Even in this, you and I can dance. But you need to let Me take the lead."

⸺ ✻ ⸺

The Lord, your eternal dance Partner, will take you where you've never been and show you things you've never seen. Many years ago, while I was still single and serving on staff with Campus Crusade for Christ, I received an invitation from Josh and Dottie McDowell to go with them to Hawaii. That was an offer I couldn't refuse! I was so excited to go to the island of Kauai.

One day after we had arrived, Josh took us for a drive around the island. As we drove along a winding road, he said, "Catherine, wait until you see what I'm going to show you." I had no idea what he was talking about, but I trusted Josh. If he had something exciting in mind, I knew it would be worth seeing.

Finally, after what seemed like a long time, he brought the car to a stop and said, "Okay, everyone out. We're here." He walked on ahead to the edge of a cliff, and the rest of us followed. When we reached the edge, we knew why Josh had brought us to that place—we were gazing at the beautiful Waimea Canyon, the Grand Canyon of the Pacific. If I had simply read a brochure about the canyon, I would have never chosen to drive such a long distance. But Josh knew about the destination, and we all benefited from his knowledge.

In every situation, whatever your circumstance, the Lord wants to lead. He does not intend for you to handle life by yourself. His leading is a most important part of the dance, for He is taking you on a journey to His desired destination. And along the way, He will show you a new view of Himself or of your own life. But there is a cost. This new view of the Lord is available only to those who spend time with God and have experience with Him. A.W. Tozer reminds us that the prize is worth the price: "It will cost something to walk slow in the parade of the ages, while excited men of time rush about confusing motions with progress. But it will pay in the long run, and the true Christian is not much interested in anything short of that."[3]

Time with Jesus and experience with Him lead to new, life-changing discoveries. These discoveries have the power to transform you and change the rest of your life. As you dance with the Lord Jesus, you will experience new, magnificent, and majestic views of Him in all His beauty, His love, His joy, His peace, His patience, His kindness, and so much more. He changes you, empowers you, refreshes you, and moves you from within your heart. He truly does turn your mourning into dancing. And your journey with Jesus becomes an adventure— the great adventure of knowing God.

You may be thinking, *But I can't actually see Jesus. How do I experience One I cannot see?* Think about the sun in the sky. Even if the sun is hidden by clouds during the day or by the earth in the dark of night, you know it exists. We count on the sun's existence by faith. We feel its warmth, experience its work, and see its effect on the earth and in our lives. In the same way, your dance with Jesus is a by-faith experience that yields real-life results. You will "see" Him at work in and through you. He can enlighten the eyes of your heart so you can know Him better (Ephesians 1:18).

The dance is all about the heart. The heart is where the Lord engages us in an intimate exchange of love, conversation, communion, and fellowship. We respond to His overtures and are drawn into a dance where we enjoy His presence. As we dance with Him, we learn to trust, love, pray, endure, hope, and grow. These qualities teach us more about the dance, enabling us to follow the Lord's lead through more demanding steps and movements. The movements tell the stories He is writing in the chapters of our lives.

He is constantly designing, fashioning, and shaping our lives, for He is the Master Designer. All along the way, regardless of the obstacles we face, the Lord holds our hearts in His hands. Sometimes we may feel as though we are abandoned, shivering in the cold wind of the dark night. But we are never alone. We are in the dance with Jesus for all eternity. And just when we least expect it, He surprises us with unexpected new steps in the dance, turning us and twirling us and leading us to wonderful new places.

So many have gone before us in the dance. The Bible is filled with remarkable dancers—men and women who drew near to the Lord and, like David, followed Him as He led them through impossible situations. We need to learn from dancers like that. I find some of the greatest dance stories in the Gospels, where Jesus invites many unique and interesting characters to dance. And in the stories of such women as the Samaritan woman, Mary (the mother of Jesus), and Martha, we understand ourselves better, and more importantly, we realize our need to engage in the dance.

I have not always known about the dance, and perhaps you haven't as well. All of us have a story of how the Lord brought us to the place where we finally responded to His invitation, *Will you dance with Me?* He's still teaching me about the dance. In every situation, I ask, *Lord, how can I possibly dance with You in this circumstance?* And then, throughout the Bible, I hear Him invite me to dance, to follow His lead, and to enter into the great adventure of knowing Him. As I share this love story of the dance, perhaps you will see more clearly the Lord's overtures in your own life. And then maybe you will move onto that dance floor with greater ease, lean into the embrace of your Lord, and dance. So put on your dancing shoes and get ready. Here we go.

2

Overture

A young girl stared through her apartment window, waiting for her father as she did every weekend. She allowed her heart's desire to surface in a whisper—"Maybe this is the day he will come." Her heart swelled, and she sighed just to think of the possibility of seeing her father drive up, get out of the car, and come to the door. She thought of him even now—tall and handsome with a big jovial smile.

But time passed, and still no car appeared in the drive. She continued waiting…and waiting. Quiet minutes became painful hours. A deep sadness began to fill her heart. This day had felt different to the little girl. A repressed thought seeped into her mind: *Maybe he won't come today. And maybe he will never come.* This devastating thought drove her from the window, and she raced through the apartment, running from room to room until she found her mother. Falling into her mother's arms, her face was wet with tears. She could not keep the great sadness inside anymore.

"He's not going to come, is he, Mother?"

Her mother closed her eyes, and tears ran down her face as well. Holding her daughter close, she said, "No, honey, he's not."

That day marked the first realization of a deep longing in one young girl's heart—a longing for eternal love, rescue, fulfillment, meaning, and redemption of a loss.

Friends, let me share a secret with you. That little girl was me. My father was the person I was longing for; my dad was the one I wanted so much. My heart was broken that day, and tears ran down my face. In that moment so many years ago, I experienced what all children experience when their parents divorce or separate. For me, the pain and loss were real. The experience was woven into the story of my life and became an integral part of my journey. The sorrow I felt then seemed to awaken me to a need that I spent years trying to satisfy. I sensed a hunger for acceptance and a desire for a love relationship that would never end.

When I was in college, I saw a movie about the life of Jacqueline Kennedy Onassis. One scene in particular is etched in my mind. Her father had come to visit her, and at the end of their time together, she stood at a second-story window and watched him leave. She waved as he got into his car and drove away. I began sobbing uncontrollably when I saw that scene. My emotional response was sudden and shocking to me. Only then did I realize the depth of my own love for my father and my need for a great, eternal love. Only then did I know how much, deep in my soul, I wanted to dance.

I walked out of the fifth-grade classroom and looked across the sidewalk to the field where we played volleyball. I saw two girls, part of the popular crowd, looking at me and laughing. A familiar feeling settled in my heart. I was on the outside looking in. As if I were standing alone out in the snow, looking through a window at friends and family sitting in front of a fire blazing in the fireplace, I felt so alone. Every day I felt this rejection clamoring for control, threatening to rule my thoughts and emotions. Now, as I look back on it, I understand. My mother was the music teacher at my grade school. And I was a hard-working student who got good grades in most subjects. Teachers love students like that, but most kids don't. And whether anyone cares to admit it, power struggles for acceptance and popularity are waged in almost every arena, even in grade school classrooms and playing fields. I just wanted to be part of the group.

I remember standing at the volleyball court, waiting to be chosen for a team. I watched as one girl after another was called to a team. I was chosen last—again. I was still on the outside looking in. And so in my first real social context, I became a people pleaser and worked hard to gain acceptance from those around me. But the eyes of One who loved me more than life itself were watching, waiting for the day when He would pull me into His arms and lead me in the most beautiful, personal, intimate dance—a dance He had dreamed of before He had commanded the stars and planets to exist.

The same One who had His eye on me also dreamed of dancing with another woman two thousand years ago. This woman, hungry for the perfect love, had searched for her heart's desire in the arms of more than one man. She had been married to five different men and now was in a new relationship with yet another. She had hoped that this time she would be loved for who she was. And the relationship may have begun well, but still she felt empty, restless, thirsty, and unfulfilled. On a day like every other day, as she went about her regular chores, she picked up her water jar and began the long walk to Jacob's well for water.

While she was walking on the dusty road, she passed a group of men from Judea making their way into town. They turned their heads, clearly avoiding any eye contact with her. Their actions didn't faze her. She was used to such disregard and lack of respect. In fact, she expected it, for she was not only a woman but also a Samaritan. As she neared the well, she noticed a man sitting by the opening where the water was drawn. *Oh no*, she thought, noticing his dress and appearance. *He's not from around here. He's from Judea.* She knew Jews had no dealings with Samaritans and especially with women. And then, looking more closely, she noticed he was clearly wearied from long travel with dust on his robe and perspiration dripping from his face. She didn't say anything, for she knew that to engage a man like him in conversation would be unacceptable. But she didn't need to say anything.

She didn't know that He was keeping an appointment that had been scheduled from eternity past. He had come to the well just to see her. In fact, He could have taken the eastern route and completely avoided Samaria. But He chose to come to Jacob's well on that day. He had seen this woman's yearning, unsatisfied, restless heart, and He wanted to give her a new heart. Why? Because He was her eternal dance Partner, and He had designed her to dance with Him. Now it was time to dance. Watching her prepare to draw water from the well, He began his invitation: "Please, give Me a drink."

The overture is the opening, initiating move. Every beautiful love story has it. The overture is the moment when the lover reaches toward the beloved in hope of a response. And with the Lover of our souls, the overtures continue again and again. He is persistent. He will have us for Himself.

Sheldon Vanauken's life was a demonstration of God's intention to dance with us. Vanauken wrote letters to C.S. Lewis with perplexing questions about God. Lewis patiently responded with brilliant answers. Near the end of his letter dated December 23, 1950, Lewis wrote, "But I think you are already in the meshes of the net! The Holy Spirit is after you! I doubt if you'll get away! Yours, C.S. Lewis." He was right. Within about four months, the spiritual fog cleared for Vanauken, and he said yes to the dance with the Lord. Lewis responded on April 17, 1951, "Dear Vanauken, My prayers are answered…There will be a counter-attack on you, you know, so don't be too alarmed when it comes. The enemy will not see you vanish into God's company without an effort to reclaim you. Be busy learning to pray...Blessings on you and a hundred thousand welcomes. Make use of me in any way you please: and let us pray for each other always. Yours, C.S. Lewis."

Our eternal Partner in the dance is tenacious. He never gives up. Even the worst cases, the impossible ones, are within His reach, all the way from heaven to earth. And let me tell you—that fact encourages me because some cases seem hopeless. I think about Saul, whose life is described in detail in the book of Acts. If ever someone could be considered a lost cause, Saul could. Here was a man who was committed to religion and filled with misdirected enthusiasm. He was well-versed in the Old Testament law but completely unschooled in its true meaning and fulfillment. He was so convinced of the blasphemy of this new group who followed One named Jesus that he felt he was doing God a favor by persecuting them.

Where did he get the idea to attack Christians? I believe one significant event must have influenced his actions. No one living in the area of Judea and Galilee at the time could have missed it. The number of believers in Jesus was growing, and one man in particular was doing great signs and wonders in Jesus' name among those in Jerusalem. His name was Stephen.

Stephen was an irritant to many of the religious leaders in the synagogue. They couldn't argue with him. His speaking was too strong and eloquent. But more than that, the leaders were no match for an unseen but very real power at work in Stephen's life—the power of the Holy Spirit. And so these men decided to falsely accuse Stephen. "We have heard him speak blasphemous words against Moses and against God" (Acts 6:11), they said, stirring up the anger of the people and those in authority.

Stephen stood accused in front of the high priest. "Are these things so?" the high priest asked. Now was Stephen's great and defining moment.

Beginning with Abraham, Stephen outlined God's invitation to His people to join in the dance. He spoke of God's overtures toward

Isaac, Joseph, the people of Israel, Moses, David, and Solomon. And then Stephen turned his attention to the religious leaders and spoke of God's invitation to them. He got personal about their response to the One who had reached out to them again and again. "You stubborn people! You are heathen at heart and deaf to the truth. Must you forever resist the Holy Spirit? That's what your ancestors did, and so do you!" (Acts 7:51 NLT).

His words penetrated with such intensity, they could stand no more. They put their hands over their ears, dragged him out of the city, and began to throw stones at him. Each stone, one after another, found its target, until finally Stephen fell to his knees, shouting, "Lord, don't charge them with this sin!" He died an agonizing death at the hands of those who couldn't stand what he had to say about God's continued overtures and their failed response.

But in the middle of this high drama, God was making a dramatic overture to one who was a disaster waiting to happen for believers in Jesus. He was a Pharisee of Pharisees who had been carefully trained by the great teacher Gamaliel. He was about to become the first-century church's worst nightmare. But God is always greater than any darkness that oppresses the earth.

When Stephen's accusers took off their coats so they could stone him, they put them down at the feet of a young man named Saul. Saul was watching everything. He was a witness, and he wholeheartedly agreed with Stephen's execution. But he also heard every word from the mouth of one who was about to step into the presence of God, one who knew how to dance and who would live in God's forever embrace. Stephen's dance with the Lord was one of God's powerful overtures to Saul. Saul didn't know it then, but one day soon he would respond to the Lord's invitation, step into His embrace, and dance with Him. Oh, how he would dance!

⁓ ❈ ⁓

Every overture by our eternal Partner is custom-designed just for us. God is interested in and even delights in every detail of our lives (Psalm 37:23 NLT). His overtures in my life have been personal and effective in drawing me straight into His waiting arms.

Excitedly, almost frantically, I ripped the wrapping paper off of my favorite kind of gift. I knew it was a book. I could tell. And at the age of nine, I could read very well, and I loved books more than any other possession. This book was a gift from my mother, and it was not your typical book. It was big and heavy. I liked that. I looked at the cover—*Marion's Book of Bible Stories*. I leafed through the pages and saw the colorful pictures at the beginning of some of the chapters. I started on page 1, looking intently at the pictures and wondering about their meaning.

"I'm going to start reading this book right away. I want to know the stories behind those pictures." The first story was all about the creation of the world. After I read that story I walked outside and looked at the sky, the trees, and the grass, and I said to myself, *God made all of this. And God made me.* The more I read from this book, the more I thought, *This book is different from any other book. These stories aren't made up—they really happened.* I read my Bible storybook over and over again. It was, without a doubt, my favorite book. And no wonder—for in it, the Lord was reaching out to me; His overtures were very real and personal.

In spite of my joy with reading Bible stories, I soon discovered I had a streak of meanness that reared its ugly head from time to time. I tormented my brother and fought him for my mother's attention. Then I hid my actions of disobedience from my mother. One Sunday, my mother sent my brother and me to church and gave us money for the offering. Instead of giving that money to the church, we held on to it and bought candy at the store and ate it on the way home.

Another day a friend of mine and I took candy from the lunch bags of our softball team members. I was called in to the principal's office, where I vehemently denied doing the evil deed. Because my mother was the music teacher of my grade school, she was also called in to the office. I finally got caught in my own lies and had to apologize to the entire team. I was embarrassed and humiliated and vowed to never do anything wrong again. That resolve lasted for one day. I had a propensity for wrongdoing and could not get rid of it, regardless of how hard I tried.

I did enjoy thinking about God. Who was He really? What did His existence mean to me? These thoughts about God were not things I intentionally conjured up. God came to my mind at different times each day and tarried in my thoughts. I welcomed each new question and stopped to linger in those "God moments."

In high school, I read some information about cheerleader tryouts. I looked at the cheerleaders and thought, *They are the popular ones. If I could become a cheerleader, I would finally belong.* I was stunned when I was chosen as one of the cheerleaders. *I've arrived!* I thought to myself, reveling in what I considered to be a dream come true. Imagine my surprise when I discovered that my feelings of exclusion still haunted me. I was *still* on the outside looking in. Even though I was now a member of one of the most popular groups, I still felt so alone. I didn't belong anywhere.

One day a friend said, "Catherine, why don't you come with me to our Young Life group?" Susan and Lee Noble were the leaders of that group, and when I walked into their house, I thought, *I feel at home here.* The atmosphere was somehow different, and I now know why. I experienced the love of Jesus Christ. His love was everywhere in that house, in the lives of Susan and Lee and all the high school kids who were part of Young Life. I sat on the floor and listened to the music and a message from the Bible. I heard the invitation to dance with Someone who was more beautiful than I could imagine.

I was intrigued, but I was also afraid. I could only stand at a distance and watch. What if He was talking to someone else and not me? And what if He had something in mind for our dance that was different from my own desires? And would He leave and go away? I knew He wanted to dance with me—this Jesus was holding out His arms, inviting me to enter into His divine embrace. And I moved toward Him for a brief moment and entertained His overtures. But I was not yet ready. College was just around the corner. And so, in the end, I stepped back. And I watched from a distance this One who was inviting me to dance.

In college I was surprised with a new freedom to do whatever I wanted. *Now I'm going to have fun!* I resolved to myself. I poured myself wholeheartedly into everything that looked exciting. This direction I chose for my life resulted in aimlessness and despair. I dated guys who could never love me enough. I went to parties that never satisfied me with enough excitement. And my classes in school were boring and purposeless. I stayed up late and slept in, often missing class.

One day, early in the morning, a knock on the door of my apartment awakened me from a deep sleep. *Just go away,* I thought. But they were persistent. I threw off the covers, grabbed a robe, and opened the door. "Yes?" I asked the couple who was standing there smiling.

"Hi! We're visiting people in these apartments and just wanted to make sure we had an opportunity to meet you. We wanted to let you know that God loves you and has a wonderful plan for your life."

I thought, *That's what I need. A plan for my life.* I said, "Would you like to come in?"

For the next hour they talked to me about Jesus and His love for me, and I listened. When they spoke of sin, I remembered stealing candy as a child and being mean to my brother. I knew I had surely sinned. They explained to me that God would forgive all my sins.

"How can that be?" I asked.

"Jesus died on the cross and paid the penalty for all your sins—past, present, and future."

But I wasn't convinced. "That's impossible because my future sins are still future. How can something in the past pay for something in the future?"

Surprisingly, they had an answer for me. "Your past sins were future sins two thousand years ago."

Hmm, I thought. "Good answer."

They explained more. "It's not enough just to know what Jesus has done for you. You must receive Him into your own life. He loves you and wants an eternal relationship with you."

Could He really love me? These people talked about Jesus as if He were real and personal. "Thank you very much," I said. "What you have to say is very interesting to me, but I'm afraid. And I'm not ready to give up my way of life." I can honestly say now in retrospect that I was afraid of the unknown. My own pitiful aimlessness seemed safer than launching out into the arms of a person I could not see with my physical eyes. Have you ever known something that was right and true but not been able to grasp it for yourself and hold on to it?

After that couple left my apartment, I thought for a long time about Jesus. His overtures were making an impression on me. I didn't know it then, but my own feet were now in the meshes of the net, just as Sheldon Vanauken's had been. And I was not going to get away. A new sensitivity settled into my heart because as much as I protested to that sweet couple who dared to invade my world that day, I was beginning not to care so much for my self-serving life. Little did I realize that I was about to step out onto the dance floor and into the embrace of the One who loved me. In only a matter of months I would say, *Yes, Lord, I will dance with You.*

The uncreated, self-existent, all-loving God wants you and me for Himself. He is the relentless Romancer, pushing through every obstacle to embrace us, hold us, love us, and then dance with us. Oh, the dance! When we truly understand what God wants for us, we will no longer forget Him or run away. We will search for the One who longs for us, and we will continue to search until we leap into His arms and allow Him to lead us into the dance. When we dance with God, we enjoy the bliss of an intimate ongoing communion with Him. We relate to

Him, converse with Him, and follow His lead in the valleys and vistas of life. He knows the way even though it is hidden to us.

And so we lean into His embrace, dancing on and on through life with Him. He holds our heart with His love and compassion as only He can because He alone loves perfectly. With Him holding us safely and securely, we are free to feel, to give love to others, and to truly live the life we are meant to live. Sometimes the dance will bring tears, sometimes laughter or sorrow or pain. The dance continues through failures and many joy-filled moments. It includes big surprises, for God loves to do more than we can ask or imagine. Such is the dance with our Lord.

Our dance is like a homecoming as we step safely into the secure embrace of God's wide-open arms. Henri Nouwen described a new discovery of God's overtures and initiative in his own dance with the Lord, and he shared a unique perspective on his response to God:

> For most of my life I have struggled to find God, to know God, to love God. I have tried hard to follow the guidelines of the spiritual life—pray always, work for others, read the Scriptures—and to avoid the many temptations to dissipate myself. I have failed many times but always tried again, even when I was close to despair...The question is not, "How am I to find God?" but "How am I to let myself be known by God?" And, finally the question is not "How am I to love God?" but "How am I to let myself be loved by God?"[1]

Nouwen describes this new response to God's initiatives in his own life as a personal homecoming. I appreciate his words because although he had danced with the Lord for many years, written many books, and taught in some of the best seminaries in the world, he was realizing God's overtures in the dance in a new and deeper way than ever before. His comments ring true for me because I too am still learning to dance.

On some days, I don't want to dance. Sometimes I just get stuck.

But here is what I have discovered: My eternal dance Partner never stops. He is always holding out His hand and inviting me to dance with Him. I am learning to say yes and to enter into the adventure. And you can say yes too. Even if you, like me, have experienced loss and rejection and loneliness, you can still dance with Him. He is always holding out His hand and asking, "Will you dance with Me?" That's really what He means when He invites us to know Him in an ongoing, moment-by-moment, intimate relationship.

I wonder how the Lord has designed His overtures for your dance with Him. He may not meet you at a well and ask you for water, as He did the Samaritan woman. But He has personally and continually reached out to you and invited you to dance with Him. In eternity past, He scheduled specific times for appointments with you. Where are you in your dance with the Lord? What will your dance with the Lord mean for your life? How can you dance with Him? And what happens when you say, "Yes, Lord, I will dance"? Let's see if we can find the answers to those questions as we continue in this love story of a woman's heart that dances.

3

Yes

"Thanks for the chair," I said to the man as I shoved it back into its place at his table. A large group of my friends and I had nearly taken over the restaurant, and we had needed just one more chair. The man looked at me, scowled, and said, "Thank you for putting that back. Are you from that church down the road?"

"Yes, as a matter of fact, I am. It's a great place, and people are finding God and growing in the Lord there."

The man looked at me with disdain. "Who?" he asked without much of a question mark in his question.

"God," I replied, thinking he hadn't heard me the first time.

"Who?"

"God," I quietly repeated, now getting his point.

He looked at me with another scowl.

"You don't believe in God?" I asked.

"No, I don't believe." He couldn't even bring himself to say "God."

I said, "Let me ask you—when you go out at night and you see all those stars, what do you think about their origin? Can you make a star?"

He said with a smirk, "Yes, I can."

I replied, "Oh, give me a break. You and I both know there's no way you can command a star into existence. And yet that's exactly what God did when He made the universe."

He said, "Well, I'm an agnostic, and I don't believe in God."

"Well there is a God, and He is Creator of even you," I said. "Anyhow, it's nice to talk with you. Maybe I'll see you again sometime."

I walked out of the restaurant thinking, *Wow, what an encounter. It's not every day you have a conversation like that!* I ran to catch up with my friends to tell them what had happened. As we stood outside, talking and saying our goodbyes, who do you think walked out of the restaurant? You guessed it—my friend, the agnostic. He looked at me with his trademark scowl. "You still here?"

"Yep. I'm still here."

He looked at my Bible.

I noticed his look and the object of his interest. "You know, you might want to open the Bible sometime and find out what God has to say to you."

He said, "I read the Bible once, in college."

"But you read it as literature, didn't you. You didn't read it as a love letter from God to you."

The man looked over at a bench in front of the restaurant. "Can we sit down for a minute?"

I was shocked at his request. Here was a man who proudly declared himself an agnostic, and now he wanted to talk. So there we sat, in front of this restaurant, talking about God. He began opening up, and once he did, the words poured out. "I'm a mixed bag when it comes to religion," he confessed. "My parents were Jewish, but I wasn't raised in the Jewish religion. As a matter of fact, my friends in school were all Christians, and we had a club that met in the basement of the Methodist church. So I became a Methodist for eight years. Then I married a girl from the Bronx and became a Catholic for twenty years. When we divorced, I went back to being an agnostic."

I said, "Let's talk about Jesus. Do you believe Jesus is who He claimed to be?"

"Well, He claimed to be the Son of God, didn't He?"

I said, "He claimed to be God. God is triune—the Father, the Son, and the Holy Spirit."

He said, "Oh yeah, I remember hearing that. But I don't believe in God."

I said, "You know what?"

"What?"

"God loves you."

"How could He love someone like me? I'm not a good person."

I said, "God loves you, and He has His hand on you. I know that you think about Him sometimes and wonder."

He looked at me with surprise.

I continued. "It was no accident that we met today."

"Oh yes it was," he protested with slightly less force.

I said, "And furthermore, I can tell you this—not only is the Bible true, not only did God create the heavens and earth and even you, but I've seen Him change my life, and I've experienced Him in my own life."

He extended his hand and said, "I'm Joey. What's your name?"

"Catherine. And Joey, you know what?"

"What?"

"I'm going to be praying for you."

And the man who claimed he didn't believe in God said, "Good. Someone needs to because I surely need prayer."

I said, "Maybe I'll see you around sometime."

He said, "Maybe so."

Two thousand years ago, the venue for the Samaritan woman wasn't a restaurant, but a watering hole known as Jacob's well. The same God who was pursuing Joey the agnostic to join the dance also went out of His way to find this woman who had all but given up on any hope for a life of meaning and significance. She had known the fleeting intimacy of at least six men but had not found her one true love—someone who would love her unconditionally, not because of who she was but in spite of all her shortcomings. She had not yet found the one who could place eternal commitment behind the words, *You are beautiful, and I will love you forever.*

But now, here she was, standing face-to-face with a man who had shockingly engaged her in conversation and was asking her for water. She did not know she was speaking with the One who created her. He knew her heart better than she ever would. He was the great light that had dawned in a land filled with people sitting in darkness and the shadow of death (Matthew 4:16; Isaiah 9:2). His name was Jesus. This woman on this day in Samaria was one such person in darkness about to come out into the light. For her eternal Partner, Jesus, was ready to dance, and He wanted to dance with her.

And so, thirsty and weary from His journey, Jesus asked her for a drink. She replied, "How is it that You, being a Jew, ask me for a drink since I am a Samaritan woman?" (John 4:9). She knew that Jews, in that day and culture, had no dealings with Samaritans. She was intrigued and also baffled by His request of her, regardless of His apparent personal need for water.

Ah, now the invitation to the dance had begun in earnest. Jesus had initiated. And she was responding to His overtures. In only one statement He had broken through many barriers that could have kept her from even considering the dance—barriers like racism, sexism, and economic discrimination. He immediately turned the conversation around to His true desire, which was borne out of His own nature of mercy, compassion, and grace. He was not out to get something, like all the other men she had ever known. No, He was a Giver, and He desired to give her the gift of God—living water.

He said, "If you knew the gift of God, and who it is who says to you, 'Give Me a drink,' you would have asked Him, and He would have given you living water." She asked Him where such water would come from. He told her what she had longed to hear—He had water that would satisfy her deepest thirst, and she never had to be thirsty again. "Whoever drinks of the water that I will give him shall never thirst; but the water that I will give him will become in him a well of water springing up to eternal life." Jesus knew the deepest unmet desires of her heart. And He longed to answer them with Himself.

She had heard enough. "Sir, give me this water, so I will not be thirsty nor come all the way here to draw."

Jesus knew she would dance. But He was not quite ready, for she had to know He knew her, everything about her, and that He loved her still. He said, "Go, call your husband and come here."

She replied, "I have no husband."

There is no mistaking His response. "You have correctly said, 'I have no husband'; for you have had five husbands, and the one whom you now have is not your husband; this you have said truly." He knew her through and through, all the way to her heart. God sees beyond the outward appearance into the heart. For that is where the dance begins—in the heart. It would have been one thing to have had one or two husbands, but five! And here was a man who had never met her, and He knew! She must have been devastated to know she could have no masks in the presence of this man. The veneer was off, and the walls were down.

She tried to change the subject, "Sir, I perceive that you are a prophet. Our fathers worshiped in this mountain, and you people say that in Jerusalem is the place where men ought to worship."

Jesus took advantage of her attempt to distract Him from His purpose and spoke of the inner nature of the dance: Worship comes from within. "God is spirit, and those who worship Him must worship in spirit and truth." Jesus now arrived at the heart of the dance, and in doing so, He pointed out to this woman that there was so much more for her in life than she had known. He continued engaging her in conversation, even theological discussion, demonstrating His interest in her, His sense of dignity and respect, and His compassion for her in spite of her own sin.

We don't know everything she was thinking, but we can assume she must have been wondering, *Who is this man? He has to be more than a man to know all about me, even the secret things that no one knows.* And so she brought up the topic of the Messiah. "I know that Messiah is coming (He who is called Christ); when that One comes, He will declare all things to us."

What a moment for Jesus. And what is so amazing is that He revealed His identity not to the heads of the government or the religious leaders, but to a Samaritan woman known and loved by no one. He said to her the words she surely never forgot for the rest of her life: "I who speak to you am He." Just think—she looked into the eyes of Jesus, the One who "is near to the brokenhearted and saves those who are crushed in spirit" (Psalm 34:18). He had found just such a broken vessel, unnoticed by most, standing alone, and He wanted to dance with her.

She couldn't say no to the King of kings, the Lord of lords. She leaned in, surrendered, and said yes to His invitation to the dance. Her embrace of Jesus in the dance is oh, so clear because of the abandoned water jar by the well. One of the first witnesses testifying about Christ was a Samaritan woman who knew she was forgiven. She left her jar, ran into the city, and told everyone, even the men, "Come, see a man who told me all the things that I have done; this is not the Christ, is it?" Her testimony was effective. Because of her yes to Jesus in the dance, everyone from the town came to Jesus to find out more about Him.

When one person accepts Jesus' invitation to dance, hundreds or even thousands of lives are touched. And those who seem least likely to say yes are often the ones whose dance is most influential. Such was the case of Saul. He had heard Stephen's powerful testimony about Jesus and had watched as Stephen was stoned to death. Saul heartily agreed with the treacherous actions of those who persecuted the early church. In fact, Saul became one of the most feared persecutors and even thought he was pleasing God in his zealous hate. But then came the momentous day when Jesus was ready to dance with Saul. Jesus' invitation was sudden, swift, and spectacular.

As Saul traveled on the road to Damascus, a light from heaven flashed all around him. Saul fell to the ground and heard the voice of his eternal dance Partner saying, "Saul, Saul, why are you persecuting Me?" (Acts 9:4).

Saul asked the important question, "Who are You, Lord?"

"I am Jesus, whom you are persecuting, but get up and enter the city, and it will be told you what you must do." Apparently, hearing the voice of Jesus was enough for Saul to say yes to the dance. Amazingly, he changed from a persecutor of the church to an evangelist and teacher of the church, wanting to know about nothing in life but his eternal dance Partner, Jesus Christ.

When you say yes to the dance with the Lord, your life is never the same. Saul became Paul and was chosen by Jesus to share the gospel with Gentiles, Jews, and even kings (Acts 9:15). Paul's dance with Jesus has influenced millions to this day.

When the couple from Campus Crusade came to my apartment that day to tell me about Jesus, they made the invitation to dance very clear and even engaging. I knew He wanted to dance. I sensed that His embrace was waiting for me. But I still held my distance. My freedom in college to do whatever I wanted was an unexpected surprise. I took advantage of it and spent a lot of time in the pursuit of play and fun. As I shared before, this direction I had chosen for my life resulted in aimlessness and despair. I was very much like the woman at the well, with a deep thirst in my heart that nothing had satisfied.

I lived in an apartment with three of my friends from high school. I was the wild one, and they constantly reproved me to straighten out my life. One day, the captain of our high school cheerleading team visited us. I looked at her and thought, *Why can't I have a life like hers?* She was committed to Jesus, and yes, she danced with Him. Oh, how she danced. Just seeing her again was enough to move my attention to the Lord's invitation to me so many years ago. After she left that day, I thought, *Where is my life going? What in the world am I doing? What would happen if I did step from this way of life into the arms of Jesus and let Him lead me in life?* Those thoughts were astounding to me, and yet I welcomed them without even knowing why. Little did I know how close I was to joining in the dance.

Soon after that day with my friend, I went to a party that lasted into the early morning hours. I fell into bed exhausted and awoke the next morning with episodes of my aimless days rolling through my mind like a movie. I watched scene after scene, realizing with increasing intensity the futility of my life. Just then, I received an invitation from Someone I could not refuse. His direct approach stunned me. His invitation was clear. His words in John 14:6 reached into the depths of my very heart: "I am the way, and the truth, and the life; no one comes to the Father but through Me." He seemed to be saying, *Catherine, it's time for you to come to Me and let Me lead you in life. I want you. All of you.*

I knew it was Jesus and that He wanted me to dance with Him. And yet I could hardly believe He was addressing me. His arms were stretched wide, extended seemingly just for me. He seemed to single me out as if I was the only one in a room of millions of people. That's how special He made me feel. At first I resisted Him, afraid of what saying yes might mean. But He wooed me until I could not escape Him. And finally I grabbed His hand and found myself firmly grasped already. I said, *Lord, You are the way, the truth, and the life. To live for anything or anyone else is to live for a lie. Take me, Lord, and make me the kind of person You want me to be. I'm Yours.* I leaned into His embrace to discover a love that finally filled my empty heart. And in His gentle but firm embrace, following His lead, I began to dance with

Him. I was no longer on the outside looking in—I knew I belonged to Him. We were together forever.

I walked out of my bedroom that morning and said to my room-mate who was a Christian, "I've just given my life to the Lord." I thought she was going to faint. Her eyes widened, and her jaw dropped. I was the last person anyone would have expected to give her life to the Lord. And yet I had. I was serious. I had said yes to Jesus. It was the most exciting time for me. I called up the guys I had been dating and said, "I'm sorry, but I don't want to date you anymore. I've given my life to Jesus." Of course, they thought I was crazy. And I was— crazy in love with Jesus! I had no desire to look back at my old way of living—I was now dancing with the Lord. I called up a girl I knew who was a Christian and asked her if I could go to church with her. Then I asked her if she would show me how to get closer to Jesus and how to know Him better.

I loved this new adventure of my dance with Jesus. I had barely stepped onto the dance floor and leaned in to His embrace. He knew exactly how many steps I could handle and how far to take me in this new dance. Two things happened immediately as we began to dance together. I experienced His love, and I was set free. Oh, how I was set free!

The best way I can tell you about the impact of the love of Jesus in my life is to share one of my favorite moments in the movie *Ben-Hur*, based on the novel by Lew Wallace. If you haven't seen this movie, you need to find a way to see it. In this story, Judah Ben-Hur was part of one of the prominent families in Jerusalem. Ben-Hur was against the oppression by the Romans in that area at that time. One day, he was on the roof with his sister, watching the Roman army pass by. His sister accidentally knocked one of the tiles to the ground. The falling tiles scared the horses below and caused one of the Roman soldiers to fall from his horse. The Roman army stormed the house and arrested all of them, and Ben-Hur was sentenced to slave labor. He was forced to walk miles and miles in the desert in chains, seemingly abandoned and hopeless. No one even knew he was alive. In effect, he had lost his life. As he walked along, he became so desperately thirsty that he finally felt he could go no farther. Falling to the ground, he cried out to God.

And here is the moment that means everything to me. The shadow of a man moved across his fallen body. Judah Ben-Hur sensed the presence of Someone. He looked up and saw an outstretched hand with water. He grabbed the cup, gulping the water. And then he stopped and looked up to see the source of this singular kindness in his wasteland of despair. Studying the face of the one who found him there in the desert, he saw eyes filled with love. They were the eyes of One who was more than a man—he was looking into the eyes of Jesus.

In that moment, Judah Ben-Hur tasted heaven's world in the touch of Jesus—love, goodness, kindness, justice, and righteousness. The guards immediately came and forced Ben-Hur to get up and keep walking. But he could not take his eyes off of Jesus. And in this brief encounter, Ben-Hur was changed. He rose with a new strength and new hope. He could endure the hell his life had become. That's the power of the love of Jesus.

I too was surprised by the love of Jesus. I didn't expect such unconditional acceptance. His love is called *agape*. John says in 1 John 4:8 that God is love—it is the essential nature of God Himself. Other kinds of love involve the emotions and the heart, but agape love encompasses the mind and the will. It is a pure affection for another that imparts value and worth, prizing and protecting that one. It is a choice, a decision, a commitment. Agape love never gives up. Agape love always believes the best. Agape love always acts on behalf of the other to give what that one needs, no matter what. Agape love gives at all costs, even to the death. Agape love lasts forever.

Can you imagine the difference love like that can make in your life and mine? Let me tell you what His love did for me. His love set me free. Free from pleasing people and working hard for their acceptance.

Free from needing satisfaction in my work. Free from always comparing myself with others and falling far short. I could now exclaim, "It's gone. The feeling of inferiority, the lack of self-worth. I no longer feel like I'm on the outside looking in! I'm free! I'm free!"

The experience of Jesus' love led to my freedom. His love has continued to free many others, including Sergei Kourdakov, an agent for the KGB who was trained to persecute Christians. His modus operandi was to break in to Christians' secret meetings and beat them. Sergei participated in many of these brutal raids. For some reason, he began thinking about these Christians and the way they responded to the beatings with love, dignity, and faith in Jesus Christ. One day, he laid down his own weapons, turned his heart over to the King of kings, and entered into a relationship with God. His life was forever changed. He was set free from hate and entered into the boundless love of Jesus Christ.

Jesus set me free with grand purpose—so I could dance with Him. He had to loosen the shackles that held my heart so it could be free to dance. And dance it would—but only in His time and in His way. I was only just beginning to step into the dance with Him. I was so excited to engage in the adventure, but my heart was set free. Free to dance and dance and dance.

I'm amazed that I took so long to say yes to the dance, but I'm so glad I finally surrendered to Jesus. The most significant step on my part was taking time to think about His invitation. I seriously considered His words in John 14:6: "I am the way, and the truth, and the life; no one comes to the Father but through Me." I decided to address His statement, deal with it, and make a decision. I recognized that Jesus was looking me in the eyes, speaking directly to me, and inviting me to something much greater than my own self-destructive ways. I took His words personally.

We all must do the same and take what Jesus says personally. I thought about His exclusive claim—He is the only way to God. He said He is the truth—to follow any other way of life is to live a lie. He said He is the life—money, success, and fun will never give me real life. Those words struck at the heart of my own questions about life. I realized that Jesus was saying God exists, He desires a relationship with me, and that through Jesus I could experience a relationship with God that leads to life—meaning, purpose, and fulfillment.

Josephus, a first-century Jewish historian, wrote a massive chronicle of the history of Israel and included these facts of history: An amazing person named Jesus lived in the area of Galilee. He performed amazing miracles and astounded all who came into contact with Him. And He made the amazing claim to be the Son of God! The religious leaders of the day were actually waiting for a Messiah, a man from God. But they expected Him to come as a political king who would align Himself with them and give them power. Jesus offended these religious leaders by associating with people of ill repute, people who were poor, people whom they considered sinners. But the Jewish leaders were offended even more by His claim to be God and His offer of forgiveness of sins and eternal life.

Though these claims repelled the Jewish leaders, they drew masses of other people to Him. And as people came to hear His words, Jesus astounded them. He would touch someone who was paralyzed, and that person would walk. He would touch a prostitute, and as tears came to her eyes, she would be filled with the desire to be holy and righteous and good. He would place His hands on the eyes of one who was blind from birth, and for the first time, that one would have sight. And during parts of his three-year earthly ministry, virtually the entire area of Judea and Galilee flocked to be with Jesus. But the religious leaders plotted to kill Him, not because of what He did, but because of Who He claimed to be—God.

Larry King was asked whom he would most like to interview from across history. He named Jesus. He said, "I would like to ask Him if

He was indeed virgin born, because the answer to that question would define history." Larry King, how right you are.

Could it be that indeed, God has visited us on earth—that Jesus is indeed God? Why would He do that? Suppose with me that there is a God who is Creator, One who created the heavens, the earth, and you and me. And suppose He created human beings, you and me, for a purpose. And that purpose was simple: He wanted a love relationship with them and with you and me. Suppose His desire was to dance with us in an intimate relationship. Imagine that in the beginning, that relationship existed. Consider that when God created the first human beings, the relationship was idyllic, and the fellowship and the exchange of love between God and His creation were perfect. In short, they danced. That idyllic existence included boundaries that God Himself set up to allow for this love relationship to flourish. The boundaries were basic: God's creation was not to exist independent of Him, but was to be dependent upon Him as the source of everything.

And then one day, God's human beings crossed those boundaries. They decided on their own, with the help of one who was bent on destroying their relationship with God, to make a choice that was independent and directly against what God had commanded. Once they crossed that boundary, sin entered the world. Now suppose with me that when sin entered the world, the love relationship with God was affected. Adam and Eve's sin separated them from a holy God, and they could no longer enjoy this intimate fellowship with Him for which they were designed. They could no longer dance.

This sin created a great uncrossable chasm between man and God and affected all of mankind. The Bible tells us that all have sinned and fall short of the glory of God and that the sentence or penalty for sin is death (Romans 3:23; 6:23). Now let us suppose again that God saw man's inability to reach Him because of sin, so He reached down to man and determined to pay the penalty for sin Himself.

History records that the Jewish leaders arrested Jesus at night, secretly tried Him, and enticed the Romans to publicly crucify Him on a cross.

While Jesus was on the cross, His followers mourned. His disciples had fled, fearing for their own lives. While dying on the cross, Jesus cried out, "It is finished." These three words have defined history and made the dance with God possible and eternal. Jesus finished paying the price for every one of our sins, making possible our freedom and our forgiveness.

But His disciples didn't understand—at least not yet. His death devastated those who knew and loved Him. Three days later, something happened—something that Jesus had promised would happen. Josephus continues his story, telling us that after three days, Jesus rose from the dead. He appeared to His disciples and more than 500 others.

My conclusion after considering the claims of Jesus was that Jesus is who He claimed to be and that God has spoken in Jesus. That morning at the end of my third year in college, the Lord seemed to have met me face-to-face. I realized that if Jesus is the truth, then to live for anything or anyone else was to live for a lie. I thought through the life of Christ, His claims, and His resurrection from the dead. It would have taken more faith and less substantiated faith to reject the words of Christ than to receive them.

And so I said yes to Him and made the best decision I ever made. And it's the best decision you could ever make. What will lead us to surrender and step into the embrace of Jesus, saying yes to Him? Only He knows the ways He will personally reach out and make overtures to you, longing to hear you say, *Yes, Lord, I will dance with You.* But know this, dear friend. He wants you more than anything else. And He never gives up. He continues, tenaciously and repeatedly, to reach out to you again and again in every circumstance throughout your life. And when you finally say yes to God, you can simply pray, *Lord Jesus, I need You. Thank You for dying on the cross for my sins. I want You to come into my life, forgive my sins, and make me the person You want me to be. Lord, I want to dance with You.*

Those words are music to heaven's ears, and according to the Bible, even the angels rejoice when you accept the Lord's invitation to dance. After you say yes to Him the first time and enter into the adventure, you will hear the Lord inviting you to new steps and movements in your dance with Him. The first yes is never the last yes, for you have begun a forever relationship with the Lord. The dance is ongoing, and you will say yes again and again as He leads you. He loves your yes to Him at every turn in the dance.

I think of my friends Debbie and Ann, who prayed for years for their mother to enter into the dance with the Lord Jesus. But their mother always said no, she wasn't interested. Then she became very ill. Debbie and Ann again talked with their mother about Jesus' invitation to enter into the dance. Their mother listened, but she said, "I'm not ready." Disappointed, they left their mother's room brokenhearted.

A few days later, they visited their mother and detected something different in her countenance. They asked, "Mother, are you ready to say yes to Jesus?" She looked into their eyes and said yes. Together they prayed, and their mother stepped into the embrace of her Lord. Two days later she stepped from time into eternity, face-to-face with Jesus.

It's never too late to say yes and enter into the dance. We were born to dance with God, to move through life in His embrace, follow His lead, and experience all of Him—His love, mercy, grace, peace, kindness, compassion, joy, and oh, so much more. Eternity is set in our hearts, preparing us for the indwelling of the triune God—our Father (whom we call *Abba,* or Papa), Jesus, and the Holy Spirit—so we can dance with Him. And until we enter into the dance with Him, every possession, experience, or relationship, regardless of how wonderful, will leave us wanting more. I'm sure you have discovered the truth of that inner restlessness already. Only God is big enough to fill a heart. And when He makes His home in you, put on your dancing shoes because you are going to dance and dance and dance. Oh yes, dear friend, you are going to dance.

YES
to tomorrow.
fresh dreams.
higher mountains.
greater impossibilities
wider sunrises.
stouter courage.
braver risks...

YES
because Jesus is the divine Yes.
because He changes everything.
He is my highest Fulfillment.
He's made me whole...
takes the bad and turns it to good.
He is my Song...
my Reason to live.
for to me, to live is Christ.[1]

Ann Kiemel Anderson

4

Partners

From high above the stage, I leaned forward in my seat to look over the railing and down at the crowd, excited and filled with anticipation. Many ten-year-old girls would never have an opportunity to attend such an expensive performance or even appreciate it if they did. But my mother saved up money for months and worked extra jobs at the church so she could afford the tickets. She knew what this performance would mean for her little girl, who dreamed of being a ballerina. I sat in the velvet theater seats, staring down toward the stage, waiting eagerly for the curtain to rise on a rare appearance of the greatest ballet dancers in the world: Margot Fonteyn and Rudolf Nureyev. I could not wait to see them perform some of their most famous dances in the very best and most beautiful ballets.

Fonteyn and Nureyev may well be the greatest ballet dancers in history. No one has ever matched the beauty or precision of their moves. They reached the height of their abilities when they danced together. Nureyev was 20 years younger than Fonteyn, and he mesmerized audiences with his spectacular leaps and turns. His passionate temperament and flamboyance made him a phenomenon. The turning point of his career came when he was invited to London to dance *Giselle* with Fonteyn, already the greatest ballerina in the world.

Theirs was the most famous partnership in the history of ballet. The tension that came from the 20-year gap in their ages, their opposing temperaments, and their totally diverse backgrounds electrified the atmosphere whenever they appeared together. He was fiery and passionate. She was elegantly mature. They moved together with perfect precision as though made for each other.

And there I was, sitting in an elegant velvet seat at the theater on the west end of Phoenix, just a young girl, ready to watch something I knew I would never forget. The music began. The curtain rose. My heart beat just a bit faster. I leaned forward, looking down on the stage. Fonteyn entered from stage left. Adorned in a beautiful white filmy dress, she began moving with the music, her arms seeming to flow as one with her body. The ovation from the crowd when she made her entrance drowned out the music for a few moments. I could not take my eyes off her shoes. They were laced perfectly, and she danced on pointe. I knew someday, when I was older, I would wear toe shoes like hers. That was my dream.

Fonteyn's grace-filled movements seemed effortless. I watched her move from one end of the stage to the other. Then she stopped on the stage and slowly turned. The music heightened. And from the right came Nureyev, leaping higher than I could imagine. The atmosphere became electric as he approached Fonteyn. They began dancing together, Nureyev lifting Fonteyn and both moving in perfect precision as though dancing on air. The hours were as minutes for me. Soon, the entire performance was over, with both Fonteyn and Nureyev answering one curtain call after another.

I have never forgotten what I was privileged to see that day so many years ago. Fonteyn and Nureyev created a beautiful dance when they partnered together in the ballet. But is theirs truly the greatest dance partnership of all time? I have discovered an even greater dance partnership, an eternal one. The dance comes from a match made in heaven and includes you and me. The partnership is between you and the Lord, and when you join your life with His, you will dance like never before.

Some people merely walk through life, taking steps as they move from one event to another in a seeming cacophony of meaningless occurrences in life. But in rare instances, some will hear God's invitation, take His hand, and move in one accord with Him, following His lead throughout their lives. In ballet, every move in the dance tells a story. In the same way, when you move through life with the Lord, He tells a story in and through you to the world.

When the Samaritan woman walked along the dusty road to the well, she did not realize that this apparently routine day would be transformed into the defining moment in her life. She did not know she was about to meet the Messiah and find the answer to all the deepest questions of her heart. You already know how powerfully exciting her encounter with Jesus was. But now I want you to go deeper with me into the dance between Jesus and this seemingly insignificant, hopeless woman from Samaria. What you think about now will help you follow Jesus in the dance.

Jesus' trip through Samaria reveals at least four things about your eternal dance Partner: first, His intense desire to transform lives. John makes a point to tell us that Jesus *had* to go to Samaria (John 4:4). Know this, dear friend: When the Lord sets His sights on you to dance, He will go to extreme measures to reach you. In Jesus' day, Jewish people used a more common route from Judea to Galilee that enabled them to avoid any contact with the Samaritans, whom they considered unclean. So why did Jesus need to go to Samaria? He knew of a woman there with a heart that was hungry for the Messiah. And He wanted to answer the deepest cry of her heart with Himself. Similarly, why must He go to the area where you are? He sees into the depths of your heart and desires to dance with you there.

Second, Jesus' meeting with the woman at the well demonstrates His intricate plan and determined purpose in her life and in your life.

This woman had been married to five men and was now living with another man. She was clearly an outcast in her town. She went to the well at noon, the hottest part of the day, in order to avoid contact with other women who normally visited the well for water in the cool of the evening. And yet there was Jesus at the well, waiting for her, knowing she would come at the appointed time. Jesus is not mysterious and coy, hiding His true feelings. He wears His heart on His sleeve, so to speak, and His heart is one of great love for you. When Jesus invites you to dance with Him, He has planned and prepared for that meeting for a long time and has looked forward to the encounter, for He is ready to dance with you.

Jesus knew He was going to meet with Paul on the road to Damascus. Jesus knew He was going to invite me to dance that morning when I was in college, and He had planned every overture that led to the day I said yes to Him. And you need to know He has a plan and a purpose for you to dance with Him. Count on it—and look for His overtures in your life.

The ways He can reach out to you are infinite. When you least expect it, He will bring a thought about Himself into your mind. He may bring someone into your life who shines with His love. He could bring a book or a Bible verse your way that shows Him to you. He may show you the beauty of God in a sunset or a breathtaking view. Keep your eyes open and look for Him, and I promise you, you will see Jesus.

Third, Jesus' conversation with the woman at the well shows His love and respect for a woman who had no respect from anyone else on earth. Jesus doesn't judge you according to other people's opinions and actions. He looks at you with eyes of love, not condemnation. He designed you and knows your heart. He saw that the Samaritan woman was very intelligent but had been deeply hurt by the rejection and condemnation of her lovers and her peers. I'm sure she didn't grow up thinking, *I'd like to be married five times and then live with another man.* The direction her life had taken may have been as shocking to her as it was to the people who knew her.

Jesus engaged in intense and deep dialogue with this woman, and sometime during that conversation, their dance began. Jesus demonstrated great respect for the Samaritan woman in His dialogue with her. His discussion topics included knowledge of the most intimate details of her life, yet He never condemned her. He saw her deep inner thirst that no person had been able to satisfy, He appreciated her questions about worship, and He honored her expectant search for the Messiah. He knew she was bright enough to handle the diversity of such a conversation. And just think of this—Jesus revealed Himself as Messiah first to a simple, outcast woman at a well. John MacArthur calls this revelation "the single most direct and explicit claim Jesus ever made."[1] Jesus chose this woman at this time and place for His great revelation. If He revealed Himself to her, surely He is ready and willing to reveal Himself to you. Get ready! You may think of yourself as too insignificant or unnoticed to receive a life-changing invitation from Jesus. But His love for you is so great that His hand is already extended to you.

Finally, Jesus' dance with this woman indicates that He knows all about her and loves her still. His unconditional love is what finally won her and brought her into the dance. We know this because when she ran to the village to tell anyone who would listen about Jesus, she said, "Come, see a man who told me all the things that I have done" (John 4:29). Jesus did, in fact, know her secrets. The walls were down and the roof was off, and I would guess she was relieved. Regardless of what He knew about her, He still wanted to dance.

Friend, Jesus knows all about you. Imagine that you are going to go to your favorite coffee shop, and when you arrive, Jesus is there, waiting just for you. What will you find that He knows about you? He's aware of not only the obvious things but also the events, dreams, and desires that are woven into the fabric of your life. He knows the hurts that others don't seem to see or care about. Possibly you failed somewhere along the way, and your failure altered the course of your life. Now you are living with the consequences, or maybe you think the story of your life is over. No—Jesus knows all about you and still wants to dance with you. Maybe you have had to let go of many of the dreams and desires in your heart because of circumstances and events that are out of your control. Maybe you are a deep thinker, and you don't know anyone who even knows who you are deep inside. Well, dear friend, He knows, and He wants to engage in those deep conversations just with you—that's part of the dance you can have with Him.

When the Samaritan woman entered into the dance with Jesus, she was transformed and became a woman of great influence. Just think of it. The woman who came to the well at noon to avoid contact with other women was now so bold and courageous that she ran into the town and told even the men about Jesus (John 4:28). Her testimony was so effective that many of the Samaritans believed in Jesus. Her words were so persuasive and her dance with the Lord so beautiful that many wanted to meet Jesus themselves and enter into their own dance with Him. They concluded, "We have heard for ourselves and know that this One is indeed the Savior of the world."

This simple woman's influence continues to this day because John included her dance with Jesus in his Gospel, which he said he wrote "that you may believe that Jesus is the Christ, the Son of God; and that believing you may have life in His name" (John 20:31). I wonder how many have believed in Jesus and entered into their dance with Him because of this one simple woman who was brave enough to respond to the overtures of a weary traveler by a well who turned out to be the Messiah, the Savior of the world. And I wonder how many will believe and dance because you have entered into the dance with your eternal Partner, Jesus. The great ripple effect of your life begins when you say, *Yes, Lord, I will dance with You.*

Your dance with the Lord is really a Cinderella story, for He is the Prince, and you are His beloved. Don't ever let anyone tell you that fairy tales are only for children. Your Prince has come, and He wants to dance with you.

I love the story Leo Tolstoy tells in *War and Peace* about young Natasha Rostova attending her first ball on New Year's Eve in 1810. Positioned along the wall with her mother, Natasha watched as more than half of the ladies were chosen as partners in the dance. She voices her greatest fear:

> "Is it possible that no one will ask me, that I shall not be among the first to dance? Is it possible that not one of all these men will notice me? They do not even seem to see me, or if they do they look as if they were saying, 'Ah, she's not the one I'm after, so it's not worth looking at her!' No, it's impossible," she thought. "They must know how I long to dance, how splendidly I dance, and how they would enjoy dancing with me."

Listening to the music, she wanted to cry. Watching the men with their partners walk by made her feel hopeless and insignificant. Prince Andrew passed by with a lady on his arm. To further her pain, an aide-de-camp asked her and her mother to move farther back to allow more room for the dancers. Natasha was ready to cry, knowing she would never dance. Prince Andrew watched all the ladies from a distance, wondering whom he would ask to dance. Count Pierre Bezukhov came up to him and said, "You always dance. I have a protégée, the young Rostova, here. Ask her." Natasha did not know that she was about to dance with the Prince.[2]

I love this vignette from Tolstoy's *War and Peace* because of the surprise waiting for Natasha: She was to dance with Prince Andrew! She could never have dreamed of the prince grasping her waist and leading her onto the dance floor for an exquisite waltz. And I love thinking about our eternal Partner, the Prince of Peace, Jesus, King of kings, Lord of lords, reaching out His hand from heaven and choosing us for the dance. Could we ever have imagined such a surprise for our life?

That's why I envision our dance as a Cinderella story, where the Prince often chooses the least likely person to belong to Him forever. In the fairy tale of Cinderella, the Prince didn't choose the seemingly qualified sisters, but instead wanted to dance with the servant girl who swept floors and suffered injustice at the hands of others. And though we may experience difficult sufferings during our brief time on earth as we dance with Him, ultimately we know the rest of the story about our eternal life with Jesus in heaven—we will indeed live happily ever after.

When I graduated from college, I served in the Josh McDowell Ministry as a staff member of Campus Crusade for Christ. One of my favorite memories of those four years is my friendship with Josh's wife, Dottie. I was single, so I often asked her questions about marriage. Honestly, I didn't have the remotest idea of what marriage would be like, and I actually didn't believe I would ever marry. One day I said, "Dottie, I'm afraid that I'll marry a man and someday roll over in bed and look at him as though he is a complete stranger. And then I'll wonder who I'm married to."

She smiled and said, "Catherine, marriage isn't like that. The more years you are married, the deeper the waters run." She was revealing that her marriage to Josh gets deeper and better with each passing year. I've never forgotten her words, and they continue to encourage me about the blessed intimacy possible in marriage. Not everyone experiences the intimacy of marriage, but another relationship can offer a lifelong, enriching closeness—our relationship with the Lord.

I like to think of Dottie's words when I consider our dance with our eternal dance Partner. When we dance with Him through the years, our relationship with Him gets deeper and better. I think back to my first years in my dance with Jesus. I barely knew Him and was afraid to pray. I didn't know anything about the Bible. In fact, I tried to return the first Bible I ever bought because I couldn't find the book of Hezekiah in it. (The kind bookstore owner let me know that there is no book of Hezekiah in the Bible.) I had no idea where to begin in my relationship with the Lord, but Jesus had extended His invitation, and I was in the dance. For better or worse, I was on the stage, and Jesus was leading my life.

One of the first Christian books I read was *I'm Out to Change My World* by Ann Kiemel. Her adventurous stories of sharing Jesus with others were so exciting to me. I had never heard of anything like that before. She danced with Him—oh, how she danced! He led Ann to one person after another so she could share His love with taxi drivers, children, old men, hurting women.

Ann helped me understand the delights of a moment-by-moment dance with Jesus. I saw that He really does lead us in life and that we follow Him. I began to look at every situation from the perspective that Jesus was present in my life. I learned to ask, *Lord Jesus, what do You want me to do?* I talked with Him about everything I was experiencing, acknowledging His presence in my life on a minute-by-minute basis. This kind of living was different to me—I was used to running my own life, and I had surely made a mess of it. I realized in new ways that no circumstance in our lives can be considered outside the realm of His presence in our life. He is our eternal Partner—and oh, what a Partner we have. The more we draw near and dance, the more we will know Him.

When I realized that I was in this dance with Jesus every moment of every day, life became much more interesting and exciting to me. Now He was in control, and I was learning to follow His lead. I had my own ideas of how my life should unfold, of course. But I soon discovered that sometimes when He said no to one thing, He was about to say yes to something even better that He had planned for us.

I smile when I think about the time I applied for a Campus Crusade for Christ summer project in San Diego. I was attending college in Tempe, Arizona, and could think of nothing more exciting than going to San Diego for a whole summer. *Take me there now!* I thought to myself. I never doubted I would be going on that trip to California. So you can imagine how shocked I was when I received a letter that said something like this: "Thank you so much for your interest in the San Diego Summer Project. We're sorry to inform you that this project is full and that we will not be able to accept your application." I was devastated. The Lord had said no, and I didn't like it one bit. I dealt with the disappointment by surrendering it to the Lord, trusting His leading, and resolving to make the best of my summer there in Arizona. I was amazed at my response and thought, *The Lord is truly changing my heart, enabling me to move with Him as He leads me.* I was just a young girl in the beginning steps of her dance with the Lord.

One week later I received a phone call from a man who said, "Catherine, how would you like to go on another Campus Crusade summer project? It's not in San Diego, but somewhere else."

"Where is it?" I asked.

"Honolulu," he replied.

I said, "You mean Honolulu, Hawaii?"

"Yes."

I was absolutely floored, but now I know the Lord Jesus does things like that. Just when you think life is over or things aren't happening the way you'd like, He surprises you with something from another direction. I have learned the obvious after so many years. He has plans and ideas in His mind that have not yet entered my mind. We may laugh when we admit that we think and act as if we know all the possible options, but we really are like that. We often assume that we know all there is to know. So we fret and worry and cry with disappointment when in actuality the Lord may have a surprising new move in our dance just around the corner. For me, that summer, it was all about going to Hawaii. And what an adventure the Lord took me on there. I learned in unusually exciting ways how to follow the Lord's lead daily in my dance with Him.

I worked during the day in a hotel lobby selling pineapples, papayas, and coconuts to the tourists who were visiting from everywhere in the world. One day a young girl walked up to my booth. She and I began talking, and I asked, "Has anyone ever talked with you about having a relationship with the Lord?"

She said, "Oh yes, my mother's a Christian. She's just about given up on me, I think."

I said, "Well, it's always too soon to give up. I'd love to talk with you about how you can know the Lord."

Surprisingly, she looked into my eyes with great interest. "Okay." And with that, we spent the next half hour talking about Jesus.

Finally I said, "Would you like to pray and invite Jesus into your life?"

She looked at me with tears filling her eyes. "Yes, I would."

And so I pulled out my little sign that said "Be right back," and we walked over to the side of the hotel lobby and prayed together, talking with Jesus about her dance with Him.

After we prayed, she said, "I can't wait to tell my mom. She is going to be amazed."

Another day, while riding on a bus, I saw an older man sitting all by himself. I asked him, "Would you mind if I sat next to you?" He shook his head, and I sat down. As we started talking, I found out his name was Daniel. I asked, "Daniel, has anyone ever talked with you about having a relationship with the Lord?"

"No."

"Would you like to hear about Him?" I asked.

"Okay, why not?" he replied.

So I shared Jesus with him. Then I asked, "Would you like to pray and invite Jesus into your life?"

"No, I'm not ready for Him. I can't make that kind of decision right here, right now."

So as the bus pulled up to my stop, I said, "Nice meeting you, Daniel. I'll see you around."

The next day I went by myself to the beach for some quiet time with the Lord. I spread out a blanket and set my books and journal down. Then I just sat back and started watching all the people on the beach. Who do you think I saw? Daniel! I called out, "Daniel! Daniel! Remember me?"

He looked at me, his eyes wide with surprise. "I can't believe I'm seeing you here. I'm so glad. I want to talk some more about what you shared yesterday."

"Okay, let's talk." After a while, I asked, "Daniel, would you like to pray and invite Jesus into your life?"

This time he was ready. "Yes, I would." And so there we were, two people who were unknown to most others in the world, having a private conversation with Jesus. Only the Lord could arrange for Daniel and me to meet on that beach that day. But that's what Jesus does when we dance with Him. He orchestrates the most amazing situations, never by chance, always by His design.

Those days in Hawaii were only the beginning of a dance I've known with the Lord for many years now. I've known tremendously exciting days and also very difficult days. What stands out to me is my eternal dance Partner, Jesus. The more I dance with Him, the more I know and love Him.

Who is this Jesus, our eternal dance Partner? He is more than a man—He is the Son of God, the second person of the triune God. And He is strong and determined, our mighty warrior and dread champion (Jeremiah 20:11) and One who always overcomes in every situation. Just think of it: He gave His life for you, His partner in the dance. No one will ever love you like He does. You can count on Him. Sometimes you may not know what He is doing, but you can trust Him to hold you and carry you through even in the darkest nights. Nothing daunts Him.

He is never worried about what He is going to do. You may be panicked, but He is not. He knows what pain feels like, for He was nailed to the cross and died for us. He knows the emotion of grief and has felt tears roll down His own face. He knows what fatigue means to the body. He knows what is in our heart. He knows what we think, what we dream of, and what we desire most in life. He knows our disappointments, our failures, and our sins. His commitment to us is certain, and His love for us is strong and sure. He is dependable, lovable, and capable. He is all-powerful, all-knowing, and all-encompassing. He is what our life is all about.

A young girl who was new to our women's ministry at church came to me and asked, "Will you pray with me?"

Of course I replied, "Sure, I'd love to." I was immediately drawn to her—she was on fire with love for Jesus. I could just see Him shining from within her.

With tears in her eyes, she told me her story. She had suffered much and was recovering from addiction. She said, "Catherine, the Lord Jesus found me and changed me. I'm a new person. I've been afraid, but I'm not afraid anymore." I smiled and we prayed together.

And that's what Jesus does. He replaces our fears with His strength, His boldness, and His courage. Fear, worry, pride, and sin can keep us from dancing with our eternal dance Partner. But instead of running away, if we will draw near and lean into His embrace, we will find that He replaces our fears with His courage. He enables us to trust His promises instead of worrying about our circumstances. He replaces pride with His humility, and He applies His forgiveness to every sin. That's our Jesus—that's what He does, and you can count on Him to be faithful to you.

A young man wrote to me about his experience meeting his eternal dance Partner, Jesus. He was a drug addict and was ready to take his own life. He had lost his marriage and just about everything else. He was so desperate that he went to church to see if he might find an answer there. This time church was different for him. The preacher was out of town, so instead of having a sermon, the church played a video message from my series on the Holy Spirit, *Set My Heart on Fire*. In the young man's letter to me, he described his experience when he arrived home:

> All of a sudden I was on my face crying out, "Lord, I'm an addict. I can't do this on my own. Please help me. I'm an

addict." Mrs. Martin, the same place that my sin left me alone in an empty house ready to kill myself is where my Savior found me and healed my sickness...God is good. He has opened so many new doors for me in ministry to help those who are going through what I went through. He has restored my marriage, and who would have ever thought He would use something as foolish as my addiction to win souls for His kingdom! He really does choose the foolish things of this world.

This young man continued by describing his dance with Jesus as a linking of his weakness and the Lord's strength. You can count on your Partner in the dance to be strong for you regardless of what you may be dealing with in life. He can handle addiction, an irreconcilable relationship, a devastating bankruptcy, and even the death of one you love. He will find you, hold you, carry you, and love you. He is the Prince of Peace and the Prince of life, and He wants to give you real life.

I'll never forget the 16-year old girl who walked up to me after I spoke. Out of a crowd of 1500 women, this young girl is the one who heard Jesus speak to her own heart. She said to me, "Catherine, when you were talking about Jesus, my heart stirred within, and when you prayed that prayer, I gave my life to Jesus. I want to live for Him for the rest of my life. And I just wanted you to know."

Overwhelmed, I said, "This is the beginning of a new life for you. The Lord has a special plan in mind just for you. He loves you. And sometimes life may be difficult, but Jesus will walk every step of the way with you." As I spoke those words, tears rolled down her face. She opened her arms wide and gave me a big hug. What a powerful moment etched in time. I saw myself in her with that familiar longing for one who would love me forever. Jesus had looked all across that crowd of 1500, and His eyes rested on the heart of a young girl who was thirsty and who was ready to engage in the dance. And now the dance had begun.

John Piper wrote about his eternal dance Partner in *Seeing and Savoring Jesus Christ*. His acknowledgments page begins differently from most:

> I owe the writing of this book to Jesus Christ. He died in my place, the righteous for the unrighteous. God counted him, who was sinless, to be a sinner, so that in him I, who am a sinner, could be counted righteous. He opened the blind eyes of my heart and brought me to faith and repentance. By his Spirit he has come to live in my heart through faith, and is slowly working his character into my stubborn will. Not only that, but this Jesus Christ created the world, including me, and holds it in being by the word of his power. Every breath I take, every beat of my heart, every moment of seeing and hearing, every movement of my mind, is owing to the sustaining grace and creative power of Jesus. All other acknowledgements and thanks are secondary and dependent on this one.[3]

Only someone who dances with Jesus could write such words. He knows his eternal dance Partner well and realizes that nothing has any meaning without Jesus.

And so it is for you, dear friend. Your life has meaning only when it becomes a dance with Jesus, your eternal Partner. So draw near to Him, lean in, and dance.

Part 2

Lord, I Am a Dancer

Reflection

M arie Taglioni was made to dance. She defined ballet, dancing
in the lead role in *La Sylphide*, an exotic story of romance and
tragedy in a Scottish setting. Before *La Sylphide*, ballet was danced in
a realistic and coquettish manner with ballerinas dressed in everyday
clothes. Filippo Taglioni, Marie's father, changed the face of ballet
when he said, "Your dancing must be imbued with austerity, delicacy,
and taste. Women and young girls must be able to watch you dancing without blushing."[1]

On the evening of March 12, 1832, the history of ballet changed
forever when the ballerinas made their appearance in the premiere of
La Sylphide in Paris. They were dressed modestly in white filmy costumes, now known as the romantic tutu, with the diaphanous skirts
allowing for free movement in the dance. Marie, in the title role, demonstrated her genius for dancing on pointes, a new kind of ballet shoe
at that time. No one had been able to dance in these new toe shoes
with much ease.

Marie changed all that. She was born to dance, designed to deli-
cately and effortlessly move on stage. She seemed to float on the tips
of the pointes, performing the most difficult moves with apparent ease
and extraordinary facility. Critics described her performance by saying,
"Her feet seem not to touch the ground...she walks on flowers without

damaging them."[2] Following her performance, Taglioni mania took over. She became so wildly popular that even Russian teacakes were named after her, and ballet slippers sold for a great price.

Marie Taglioni was made for the dance. And so are you, but your dance requires that you wear shoes of grace and glory and that you dance on the stage of life with the Lord Jesus leading you in every step you take.

Simon the Pharisee might have sent Jesus a dinner invitation that read like this:

> You are invited to dinner tonight in the company of some of the most religious and powerful men in the area. This will afford you a great opportunity to meet some of the more important and influential people and share your message with them. The food will be the finest, the décor will be elegant, and the audience will be upscale, prestigious, and elite. RSVP requested.

However his request actually arrived, Jesus answered his invitation with a yes.

Simon may have had one intention, but Jesus most certainly had quite another. And surely, when Jesus entered the house of Simon, a Pharisee, He knew He was not among His best friends. All Palestine was talking about Jesus. Who was He? Were His miracles real? Why was His teaching so different from the religious leaders'? So you can imagine that Jesus' presence in Simon's house was quite a feather in Simon's cap, and many of the town's most important citizens were probably in attendance.

Jesus entered the house of Simon, took off His shoes (as was common in the Eastern culture), and leaned toward the table, reclining with His feet stretched out behind Him. When Jesus was reclining at the table, did He feel like a lion among wolves? Was He smiling inside with excitement, knowing His own purpose and plan for the evening? Soon, He heard whispers among the dinner guests and sensed someone's presence behind Him. A new dance with an unknown but forgiven woman was about to take center stage in the house of a proud, religious man who needed to learn how to dance.

A woman who was a well-known sinner in that town, deemed untouchable and unclean, surely understood the pain of fear and hopelessness. She may have thought more than once, *I wish I could start my life over again.* But one day she heard a man tell her she was forgiven. *I'm set free from all that pain! Today is a new day! This Jesus has assured me of His forgiveness for everything I've ever done. I am loved by God.* Once she knew the forgiveness of God, she was compelled to action. *I must find Jesus and express my love and gratitude to Him. I love Him. I must tell Him.*

She learned that Jesus was going to be at Simon's house. Of all places—the house of a Pharisee, one of the most religious people around. She knew how the religious leaders felt about her and how they might respond to her presence. But this day was different, and she was not to be deterred. She knew if she could just get through the doors, she would see Jesus! Securing an alabaster vial of perfume, she headed down the road toward Simon's house. Bold and courageous, she walked through the open doors, not knowing exactly what she would face but confident in her desire to be with Him. She would have her dance with Him, and no one could stop her.

Walking into the room, her eyes scanned the faces of the many people reclined at the table. Then she saw Him. *There is the One who set me free,* she thought. As she moved toward Him, her pent-up emotion began to surface, and tears welled up in her eyes and then poured down her face. Buckets could not have held all that was in her heart—the love and gratitude was more than she could bear. She fell by His feet, soaking them with her tears and perfume and wiping them with her hair.

Simon was shocked and disgusted. "If this man were a prophet

He would know who and what sort of person this woman is who is touching Him, that she is a sinner" (Luke 7:39). The atmosphere in the room must have been electric. What would Jesus do? Simon probably thought, *I can't wait to hear what Jesus is going to say to this woman.* But Jesus didn't address the woman first—no, He would not interrupt her beautiful dance on this stage. Instead, Jesus addressed Simon, answering his thoughts before they were turned to words.

"Simon, I have something to say to you."

"Say it, Teacher."

Jesus then spoke in terms Simon could understand—money and debt. "A moneylender had two debtors: one owed five hundred denarii, and the other fifty. When they were unable to repay, he graciously forgave them both. So which of them will love him more?"

In this story, Jesus explained a world of truth to Simon. Most importantly, He contrasted two debtors—one who owed much and one who owed less. Jesus was standing in a room with those two debtors present and accounted for—the woman who was dancing and Simon the Pharisee. Simon didn't yet understand, but he responded, "I suppose the one whom he forgave more."

Jesus said, "You have judged correctly."

And now, Jesus allowed the dance to take center stage and demonstrate the truth to all who were present: Regardless of how many sins you have committed, you may be forgiven by God. Jesus turned to look at the woman as He continued speaking to Simon. "Do you see this woman?" For though they had watched her actions, they had not really seen—not the way Jesus did. And so He made the contrast between Simon and the woman crystal clear:

> I entered your house; you gave Me no water for My feet, but she has wet My feet with her tears and wiped them with her hair. You gave Me no kiss; but she, since the time I came in, has not ceased to kiss My feet. You did not anoint My head with oil, but she anointed My feet with perfume (Luke 7:44-46).

Jesus was ecstatic and over the top about this woman's actions. He loved her extravagant expression of love so much that He made her the celebrity of the dinner party. And then He unveiled her true identity to all in attendance: "For this reason I say to you, her sins, which are many, have been forgiven, for she loved much; but he who is forgiven little, loves little." He made His feelings clear to everyone: She is forgiven, and now she dances with Me.

Then Jesus turned to the woman. I love this. In fact, I think I would have fallen on my face at this point. He said very simply, "Your sins have been forgiven." Simon may have thought he was going to show off his religiosity to Jesus and impress all his friends. But in the end, the dance of a sinful woman showcased the great story, the best story, God's story with a happy ending: eternal life and forgiveness of sins. We know this is true, for all in attendance began to say to themselves, "Who is this man who even forgives sins?"

Perhaps the sinful woman thought her forgiveness was too good to be true. Maybe she needed to see Jesus one more time to confirm what she had sensed was true—that Jesus accepted her and that she was now the beloved of God. Whatever her thoughts may have been, Jesus said to her before she left Simon's house, "Your faith has saved you; go in peace." Those words must have been music to her ears! She was free…saved…forgiven…at peace with God.

You are defined not by what you do but by who you are. You are a dancer, and so am I. We are designed to dance. When I first danced with the Lord, I was far from understanding my own design or destiny. I thought, *Now I've given my life to the Lord. Where do I go from here? What is this decision going to mean for me? What does He want to do in me and through me?* Not only that, I still identified myself with my old life. I was still consumed with questions. *How can He forgive me for all that I've done? How can He ever use me for His work when*

I've lived in so much sin? I had many questions and few answers. Of course, I wanted to know the answers to all my questions at once. I soon discovered that the Lord has His own timing and leads us on this adventure of the dance one step at a time.

I remember what I thought in my first Bible study. *I don't deserve to be here. I'm not worthy. I haven't lived for the Lord the way these kids have. Their lives are perfect. Mine is not.* Honestly, that's what I thought. I put myself down in my own mind—a lot. That first Bible study helped me look in the mirror and see myself as I really am, the way God sees me.

Mirrors show us what we look like, offering a reflection of the original. Water or windows can provide reflections, but mirrors give us the best view of the original. I remember standing in front of a mirror years ago when an older woman walked by, looked in the mirror, and said to me, "Don't ever get old. It's terrible!" She quietly walked away, but I, of course, was shocked. I looked in that same mirror, wondering about a woman who was overcome with the passage of time in her life, and knowing that someday I might experience those same feelings.

My husband and I love to watch the daily ritual of a hummingbird that flies into our backyard fountain, zips over to the nearest tree, and then hovers in front of one of our windows, apparently to see its own reflection. The last time I watched this hummingbird stop in front of the window, I asked my husband, "What is that hummingbird thinking when it looks at its reflection?"

My husband replied, "Not too much. Hummingbirds don't really think like humans." I laughed, thinking about a hummingbird looking at itself.

When you look in the mirror, what do you see? I heard the story of two women who were working in our church kitchen, preparing for one of our events. One woman asked the other, "Who are you?"

The other woman responded, "I'm nobody." When I heard that story, I thought about how we all occasionally feel like nobodies. I have been with people who have made me feel as though I am nothing and nobody. They didn't care about the things I love to do like writing books and teaching from the Word of God. They measured my worth in terms of their own needs, desires, and agendas. Gradually, I have learned to reject their assessment. I have chosen to look in the mirror and view myself and my life from God's eternal perspective. Then I can say, in spite of what others may think, *Lord, it's You and me. I'm so glad that You love me. And I love the fact that we dance.* And when I have felt insignificant in the grand scheme of things, finding joy in my own dance with the Lord has moved me ten thousand steps closer to Him.

We need to be able to look into the mirror and see our own significance, design, and purpose in life. Mirrors cast a reflection. We always look in mirrors to see ourselves. But sometimes we look in the wrong mirrors and become distracted and disheartened because of what others say, how they treat us, and the way they make us think and feel. We need to look into the proper mirror in our dance with the Lord to see a true reflection of ourselves and understand who we truly are.

The Bible is our mirror, and according to James 1:22-25, when we look in it intently, we begin to see who we really are. The Bible is our most reliable source of information about our dance with the Lord, for God's Word is truth (John 17:17). Let me tell you the truth about truth. When you know the truth, you will be set free (John 8:32).

When the woman washed Jesus' feet in the presence of all those religious leaders, she demonstrated to the world that her heart was set free to dance with her Lord. The shackles of sin and shame had been broken off her heart, and now she could enter into a love relationship with Jesus. And love Him was what she did—in fact, the Lord commended her because she "loved much." You and I need to know the truth about who God is and who we are so we can dance. Without the truth, we live in a temporal world of fantasy and delusion that is promoted by a culture of sin and godlessness. God has given us the truth in His Word so we can freely dance with Him.

One of the first important decisions I made in my dance with the

Lord was to buy a Bible. The lady at the Christian bookstore helped me choose a good translation that would be easy for me to understand. I was just amazed when I began reading the Bible. I realized that God had so much to say to me. I underlined verses that were most important to me. And as I began looking into the mirror of the Word to see who I was, what I saw was not what I expected.

The reflection I saw of myself in the mirror of the Word of God revealed that I was made to dance with the Lord forever. I learned that I am a dancer, and I say that joyfully because God has made me this way. I am a dancer. He has given me the heart of a dancer. God sees all the way to the heart (1 Samuel 16:7) and ultimately desires to dwell in our hearts (John 14:15-23). I am made to follow Jesus, listening for His guidance and watching for His next step in our dance together. Much of our dance with the Lord begins in our hearts with Him, and then we live it out in our lives as we follow His lead, making God-directed choices and decisions.

Understanding my identity as a dancer helps me engage in the dance. As I look into the mirror of the Word of God, I understand that just like that sinful woman who entered Simon's house, I am a sinner, and I desperately need God, but I have leaned into His embrace and have been forgiven much. No wonder the Lord made a point to tell Simon, those in the house, and even the woman that her sins were forgiven, she was saved, and she could go in peace. He confirmed her true identity to her and everyone present.

Forgiven

The woman whose heart dances with the Lord realizes and counts on the fact that she is forgiven. When you enter into a relationship with the Lord, you are forgiven completely, always, and forever. No sin you have committed or will ever commit is left uncovered by the blood of Jesus shed on the cross for you. I know that's hard to believe when we have a mountain of sins, but it's true.

Imagine your forgiveness this way. You are standing before a judge.

All your sins—past, present, and future—are laid out and listed for all to see. The judge brings down the gavel: "Guilty!" Then he reads the penalty: "Death for all these sins!" Then, something unusual happens. The judge stands and takes off his black judge's robe. He walks around to the front and says to the bailiff, "I have paid the penalty myself for all these sins. I have died in her place."

That is exactly what has happened, my friend. According to Paul in Colossians 2:13-14, Jesus has "forgiven us all our transgressions," "canceled out the certificate of debt consisting of decrees against us," and "taken it out of the way, having nailed it to the cross." I love these promises of forgiveness and their incredibly graphic language. Just imagine all your sins written out on a piece of paper and then nailed to the cross of Jesus. When He died on the cross, His death paid the penalty for every one of your sins, for He died in your place. Think about this truth and bask in it. The resulting forgiveness made that sinful woman so overcome with love that her tears washed Jesus' feet.

Charles Spurgeon once remarked that his own forgiveness gave him reason to dance. He recalled the moment he first realized he was forgiven:

> Oh! what a sweet season is that when Jesus takes away the pain of sin. When the Lord first pardoned my sin, I was so joyous that I could scarce refrain from dancing. I thought on my road home from the house where I had been set at liberty, that I must tell the stones in the street the story of my deliverance. So full was my soul of joy, that I wanted to tell every snow-flake that was falling from heaven of the wondrous love of Jesus, who had blotted out the sins of one of the chief of rebels.[3]

Perhaps you, like Spurgeon, have felt as though you were the greatest of all sinners. How can you deal with the apparent dichotomy between your feelings and what God says? Gaze long in the mirror of God's Word and drink in every line and word. You are forgiven. In fact, the forgiveness of Jesus is what enables you to now dance with Him. So stand up, dear friend, and dance, for you are forgiven. He promises.

Free

When you look in the mirror of the Word of God, you also discover that you are no longer condemned. Early on, when I first began dancing with the Lord, I spent a lot of time thinking about my sins, and I often felt as if I were drowning in my feelings of condemnation. Then someone showed me Romans 8:1: "There is now no condemnation for those who are in Christ Jesus." When I read that verse, my first thought was, *Really? Is that true?* Then I made an important decision that helped me step into my dance with Jesus in a much more confident way. I decided to believe what God said in the Bible. If He said I was no longer condemned, then His words were good enough for me. I thought, *I'm free! I'm free! My sins really are forgiven!* Even now, when doubts crowd into my mind about forgiveness of sins and I begin to feel condemned, I think of His promise in Romans 8:1 and remember, *I'm a dancer, forgiven and set free to dance.*

Created by God

You will see as you look in the mirror of the Word that you are created in the image of God, with personality, thoughts, and feelings (Genesis 1:27). God designed you in your mother's womb and has all your days planned for you. Your existence is custom-designed by the God of the universe. Isn't that an amazing thought? And yet it's true— see for yourself in Psalm 139:13-16. The wonderful truth is that you are made by God Himself to dance with God Himself.

Chosen

When a woman who dances with Jesus looks in the mirror of the Word, she also sees a reflection of someone whom God has chosen (Colossians 3:12). We are personally and purposefully selected by God to be His. We belong to Him and are His special treasure. When I first learned that God chose me, my pain from all the grade school taunting fell away. I no longer cared about not being chosen for a volleyball team. I had been chosen to enter a palace; why should I care about not being able to enter a broken-down hut! The Lord truly released me from this pain, which had haunted me for years.

Loved

A woman who dances with Jesus and looks in the mirror of the Word also sees that she is called "beloved" by her Lord (Colossians 3:12). Not "Hey, you," but "beloved." He loves you dearly and thinks of you with great fondness. This is the great love that the sinful woman experienced at Simon's house from Jesus. No wonder she wasn't afraid to boldly storm the doors of a Pharisee's home, knowing she would see Jesus.

God's love for you is written all over the pages of His Word. He expressed His love as clearly and emphatically as He could when He gave His only Son to die in your place and mine (John 3:16). Because of His great love, you are now called a child of God (1 John 3:1). We hold our heads high, rejoicing in the light of God's love (Romans 5:11 PHILLIPS). This is the posture of a dancer. Always remember, dear friend, that you are loved.

Charles Wesley wrote a hymn expressing Jesus' wonderful love for us:

> Jesus, Lover of my soul, let me to Thy bosom fly
> While the nearer waters roll, while the tempest still is high.
> Hide me, O my Savior, hide—till the storm of life is past;
> Safe into the haven guide; O receive my soul at last.

Those words are an expression from one who truly knows he or she is the beloved of God.

A Princess

Look into the mirror of God's Word, and you will also see that you are now royalty—a princess—and your Prince is none other than the Lord Jesus. Peter says, "But you are a chosen race, a royal priesthood, a holy nation, a people for God's own possession" (1 Peter 2:9). In the book of Revelation, the church—which includes all believers of Jesus—is seen as the bride of Jesus Christ (Revelation 19:7; 21:2,9). And Paul confirms this royal relationship when he points out that husbands are to love their wives as Christ loves the church (Ephesians 5:25). So, dear friend, always remember that you are a princess, the bride of Jesus Christ. You and He dance together. I have a silver necklace with a crown that I sometimes wear to remind me that I am the Lord's princess.

Beautiful

You will also discover in the mirror of the Word that when you dance with the Lord, you are beautiful. In his arms, you sparkle and shine like a light in the dark world. The Lord has washed you clean by dying on the cross for your sins, making you holy and blameless. You are, as Paul puts it, in all your glory, "having no spot or wrinkle or any such thing" (Ephesians 5:27). You are beautiful, my dear fellow dancer. Don't ever forget that the holiness of the Lord in you shines brightly and that regardless of how you may sometimes feel, you are beautiful to the Lord.

A Saint

The Bible shows you another reflection of your relationship with God: You are a saint! In Paul's New Testament letters to churches, he rarely refers to believers by name. Instead, he calls them saints.

- "You are fellow-citizens with the saints" (Ephesians 2:19).
- Paul prays that you will "comprehend with all the saints" God's love for you (Ephesians 3:18).
- God has provided "for the equipping of the saints" (Ephesians 4:12).

- You must "be on the alert with all perseverance and petition for all the saints" (Ephesians 6:18).

What does being a saint entail? As a saint, you are holy and set apart for God Himself. Jesus is the One who has cleansed you and made you holy, setting you apart for Himself. Why? So you can dance with Him. As a saint, you wear the most beautiful gown for your dance—the brightness of holiness and purity.

Favored

Women whose hearts dance with the Lord are recipients of the wonderful grace of God. You are invited to dance with Jesus not because you came up with the right answer, not because you were the best, and not because you earned His acceptance. Your invitation to dance with Him is extended to you freely—it's a gift. He doesn't give you merely a single drop of His grace, but according to Paul, He has lavished on you the riches of His grace (Ephesians 1:8). His grace is what has saved you, redeemed you, set you apart as a saint, and given you eternal life.

Grace has often been described by the acronym "God's Riches At Christ's Expense." The grace of God gives you what you need when you need it. You are encouraged, as a dancer with the Lord, to "approach the throne of grace with confidence" so you may receive mercy and find grace to help you in your time of need (Hebrews 4:16 NIV). Women who dance with the Lord know they can run to God anytime for help because they always have His favor. That's the meaning of living in the sphere of God's grace. God never withdraws His grace and always gives it as an expression of His unconditional love.

Wealthy

When we accept the Lord's invitation to dance, we become wealthy beyond measure, for we are given the right to share an inheritance that is kept for us in heaven. This inheritance does not contain physical riches that can be devalued, stolen, or destroyed (1 Peter 1:4), but a life we will enjoy forever. Knowing about my spiritual wealth sets me free from the pursuit of temporal earthly riches.

Never Alone

Looking in the mirror of the Word reveals that we are never alone. Instead, we are indwelt by the Holy Spirit, who is with us forever (Romans 8:9). The presence of the Holy Spirit in our lives empowers us for our dance with our Lord, enables us to experience the presence of the Lord, and leads us every step of the way in our lives. The Holy Spirit also transforms us from the inside out, making us look more and more like the dancers we are.

Made for a Purpose

When you look in the mirror, you discover you are designed with magnificent pupose—to know, love, and glorify God. Your heart is custom-made to house God's Spirit and make possible an intimate relationship with the triune God. Why? Because God loves you, wants to be with you, and desires a special closeness with you. Jesus promised a blessed intimacy through the Holy Spirit, in which God (the Father, Son, and Spirit) would come and make His home with us (John 14:23).

He desires communion and fellowship with you. He wants you to know Him. In fact, He says, "Be still, and know that I am God" (Psalm 46:10). He says if you want to boast in anything, boast that you understand and know Him (Jeremiah 9:23-24). When Jesus was asked about the greatest commandment, He spoke of the priority of loving God (Mark 12:30). And Paul, in speaking of the indwelling Holy Spirit, encouraged us to glorify God in our bodies (1 Corinthians 6:20). When you dance, always keep in mind you dance with the purpose of knowing, loving, and glorifying your eternal dance Partner.

⸺ ❋ ⸺

Even though we know we are dancers, we are sometimes plagued with guilt, and we lose sight of the image in the mirror of the Word. Sometimes our guilt is misplaced because we can't bring ourselves to receive the forgiveness that is ours. In that case, we truly need to look in the mirror once again and realize who we are. Other times, though, we experience guilt because of something we've done wrong— a sin we've committed. In that case, we need to confess our sin to the Lord, agree with Him that it was indeed wrong, and receive His forgiveness.

Max Lucado describes the powerful work of confession and the grace of God in our lives:

> Confession does for the soul what preparing the land does for the field. Before the farmer sows the seed he works the acreage, removing the rocks and pulling the stumps. He knows that seed grows better if the land is prepared. Confession is the act of inviting God to walk the acreage of our hearts... And so the Father and the Son walk the field together; digging and pulling, preparing the heart for fruit. Confession invites the Father to work the soil of the soul.[4]

These are just a few of the many images I see when I look at my reflection in the mirror of the Word. Part of the adventure of my dance with the Lord occurs as He shows me new truths about who I am in Him. I never tire of opening the pages of the Bible to see myself as the Lord sees me—His dancer.

Don't ever let anyone tell you that you are less than a dancer. Sometimes I hear people put themselves down or worse, tear down someone else's life, saying things like "That person is never going to amount to anything." Friend, even if no one thought you would amount to anything, Jesus is reaching for your hand and saying, *Let's dance.* Just when you are ready to give up, Jesus, your dance Partner, says, *Come on, no more self-pity. Let's go. We're going to dance!* So never give up in your dance with the Lord. You are a dancer!

—๑ ✳ ๑—

When I watch Tiger Woods hit a golf ball, I clap my hands in amazement. About the time Tiger seems to have been overcome by obstacles, he makes the long putt and takes home the trophy. Why is he able to make such amazing golf shots? Because he is made to play golf. And so it is with you. You are made to dance, so you need to boldly step in and begin to dance with the Lord.

I recently attended a preaching conference at Harvest Christian Fellowship in Riverside, California. This epic event featured some of the great preachers of all time, including Greg Laurie, John Mac-Arthur, Chuck Swindoll, Chuck Smith, James MacDonald, Alistair Begg, and James Merritt. I sat with my friend Jan, who directs the women's ministries at Harvest Christian Fellowship. We listened intently as each speaker preached his message and taught us more about sharing the Word of God in the twenty-first century.

Jan and I both write Bible studies and teach the Word of God, and we love what God has called us to do. So we were both in our element, drinking in what each preacher said. I marveled as I watched Chuck Swindoll, a master at preaching. I often laughed with enjoyment as I listened to him preach. I sometimes stood and offered my own personal standing ovation. I thought, *Now here's a man who was made to teach and preach the Word of God. What a delight!* I noticed his apparent ease at making eye contact with his audience, revealing his vulnerabilities, authentically expressing his own relationship with God, and encouraging us to faithfully run our own race. Chuck Swindoll is a dancer—he is dancing on the stage where the Lord has led him, and he is doing what God has called him to do. I delighted to watch him dance. I want to dance like that.

When you are who God has made you to be and you live the way He has called you to live, He leads you to do what He has called you to do. We need to recognize that we don't instantly dance perfectly. We are constantly looking in the mirror, realizing who we are, and learning to live by what we see. And sometimes we struggle with the apparent dichotomy of the now and not yet.

Jennifer O'Neill, Hollywood actress and international model, seemingly had everything a woman could ever want. She was beautiful and successful in her field, starring in such films as *Summer of '42*. At a very young age, she developed a vast aching emptiness, what she describes as a hole in her heart.[5] She tried to fill the void in her life with the love of others. She experienced the trauma of eight marriages, nine miscarriages, a near-fatal gunshot wound, and three other near-death experiences. She describes how God brought her to a point of decision in her dance with Him:

> Some [things] can haunt and rob us for our entire lives like an incurable disease left undetected. Personally, I was sick and tired of being emotionally and spiritually sick and tired, and I asked God to show me how to be free. And with that I was on to my next mission...with a vengeance.[6]

She describes her struggle with forgiveness once she entered into her dance with the Lord. "We are not to hold ourselves in unforgiveness no matter what our indiscretions. Jesus has already paid the price on the cross. Yet I often find forgiving myself is the part that feels so impossible." She continues by describing her need to receive God's forgiveness by faith in obedience to His promise to her in His Word. Not only once, but continually, day by day.

But Jennifer continued to struggle to forgive people and deal effectively with events in her past. She describes herself in a trap of fury, hate, and self-loathing. Here's how she was able to realize anew her own identity as a dancer:

> I had to release it all through the power of the Holy Spirit. I had to forgive, confess, repent, and receive God's forgiveness. Finally, I gave all those people, feelings, and places of pain back to Jesus in His name! Giving it all to Jesus meant that I was not the debt holder any longer. The release felt like the

first few minutes after having a cast removed from a healed leg. Right off, I was weak and unstable without the familiar shoring up of anger and hurt, but finally I was literally "cast off," and I reveled in the victory and freedom!

I love the words *victory* and *freedom*. Jesus gives us victory and freedom to enable us to dance on with Him in life.

Jennifer O'Neill helps me understand my own wrestling with becoming a dancer with the Lord. I realize that not every part of my transformation is instantaneous. I look in the mirror and see I am a dancer. But I don't always feel like a dancer. In fact, my actions are sometimes anything but those of a dancer. I must remember that Jesus is in the process of making me more and more a woman with a heart that dances with Him. I must make a claim on what I see in the mirror about myself—I am indeed a dancer—and then I must act on it. Henri Nouwen calls this the claim of our belovedness. He speaks of our choices in life as claims of our belovedness, such as reading good books and spending our time well. He calls it the fight for our identity, one step at a time.[7]

Understanding who we are as dancers changes not only the way we look at ourselves but also the way we look at others. When you look into another person's eyes, you understand that she is also made to dance with Jesus. She may not have entered into the dance yet, but she is custom-designed to dance, just as you are. I love looking into someone's eyes and just stopping for a moment to think about her significance to God, her purpose, her belovedness. She is not a mistake or an accident—not to God. I soon feel a strong desire to fight for her dance with the Lord.

If she is lost, my prayer is that she will be found and will someday dance. She could be like the woman at the well or the sinful woman who loved Jesus so much because she had been forgiven. Maybe she is like you before you knew about the dance. And she may be pouring her life into worthless things, longing for Jesus but not realizing He is the answer. Looking into the mirror and seeing who we are will help us reach out in love to those around us and tell them about the dance with Jesus. And loving others is indeed a part of our dance with the Lord, for one of His great purposes is to seek and save those who are lost (Luke 19:10).

And so, as we look at the reflection in the mirror of the Word of God, let's resolve to claim our identity as dancers and then live like the dancers we are. This means saying no to certain activities in order to say yes to the dance. Every day, moment by moment, we must live in the Word and claim what we see as personal—meant for us as dancers—and then resolve to live by the reflection we see in our mirror. Then we will find that we are ready for the next step in our dance with Jesus. And we will be like that set-free woman who lavished her love for Jesus for the entire world to see. We will dance.

Alabaster Heart

Nothing to Thee can I bring,
Holding to Thy hand I cling.
No alabaster box have I
To break open and anoint Thee by.
I have only the heart Thou gave to me
To live, to love, to honor Thee.
Take it, my Lord, it is Thine own,
Humbly, I lay it before Thy throne.[8]

Conni Hudson

Devotion

I stood, my heart pounding with excitement, in a large mirrored room with about 20 other six-year-old girls. We all wore black leotards, tights, and soft black ballet shoes. I looked into the large mirror covering the entire front of the wall and giggled. We looked like little stick figures, angular and awkward. We were beginners, and none of us had a clue what we were in for. *I'm going to learn how to dance and become a ballerina.* Oh, I just loved that thought. I couldn't wait. I was ready to go onstage and present a performance for all to see. I didn't realize that I was not ready at all. I had much to learn about ballet.

On one side of the wall in the dance studio was a long wooden barre. *I wonder why that's here.* I soon learned that all ballet dancers begin at the barre. My dance teacher, Arnora, was beautiful—I wish you could have seen her with her blonde hair and creamy skin and long muscular legs. She wore a black filmy skirt over her leotards. *Maybe I will look like that someday.*

We watched her gracefully walk with purpose over to the barre and gesture to us. "Okay girls, line up here at the barre." I took my position, grabbing the barre with my left hand. She stood in front. "We're going to learn the five main positions of ballet—first, second, third, fourth, and fifth. Every move in ballet begins and ends with these positions." She demonstrated the positions, and we followed along.

My legs felt stretched in new directions as I worked muscles I didn't know even existed.

Then Arnora taught us how to plié, bend our knees, and then return to first position. Arnora said, "The positions of the arms and hands are most important. Hold out your hands and try to copy the way I position my fingers." I looked at the soft, graceful expression of her hands and copied them exactly. I was mesmerized with the grace and beauty of Arnora's hands. As a matter of fact, to this day, when I speak or even walk, my hands naturally express themselves in the ballet positions I learned from those hours of practice long ago in ballet class. Every week, in ballet class, we learned new exercises and dance steps.

One day, Arnora said, "I'm going to teach you a dance, and all of you will have costumes made and perform for your parents." I couldn't wait until Mother picked me up from class. "Mother, you are not going to believe it. We're going to perform a ballet dance for you!" When the day arrived for our performance, you would have thought I was the star in *Swan Lake*. I was so proud with my little tutu, white tights, and pink ballet slippers. When we performed, all the observation, exercise, and practice came together into a beautiful dance for all to watch. When we finished, we all came on the stage together and curtsied, just as Arnora had taught us. Our parents applauded. I was bursting with pride. I loved ballet and knew I was on the road to becoming a ballet dancer.

Dancing in ballet requires devotion and discipline. You cannot neglect dance class. You may not have known this, but every member of a professional ballet company takes ballet class each morning, from the most famous dancers to the newest members. Rudolf Nureyev is credited with saying, "If you skip class one day, you know it. If you skip class two days, your teachers know it. And if you skip class three days, the audience knows it."[1]

———❀———

Devotion and discipline are also essential for you in your dance with the Lord. Not long after I began dancing with the Lord, I attended a Campus Crusade conference in Arrowhead Springs, California. My Bible study leader encouraged me, "Catherine, you're going to hear a lot of speakers this week. But you're going to love one in particular. Her name is Ney Bailey, and her heart is on fire for the Lord."

Well, I couldn't wait to hear Ney Bailey speak. Just her name was intriguing to me—I had never heard the name Ney before and thought this woman must be unique. Her topic was faith, and when she began talking, I instantly was drawn to her. She spoke quietly, simply, and slowly, and every word she said was profound. I could hardly write fast enough to keep up with all she was saying.

She began with the story of the centurion whose servant was paralyzed. He came to Jesus in Capernaum and implored Him, "Lord, my servant is lying paralyzed at home, fearfully tormented" (Matthew 8:6). Jesus said to him, "I will come and heal him." Ney read this conversation to us slowly and methodically from the account in Matthew, and I followed along in my Bible. Then she stopped and looked at all of us. "Now listen to what the centurion said to Jesus. 'Lord, I am not worthy for You to come under my roof, but just say the word, and my servant will be healed.'" I can still hear Ney's voice emphasizing "just say the word."

Then she pointed out how impressed Jesus was with the centurion's response. "'Truly I say to you, I have not found such great faith with anyone in Israel.' What was it about the centurion that defined his faith as great? He told Jesus to 'just say the word.' Here we have a definition of faith. Faith is taking God at His Word." My heart stirred when she defined faith as taking God at His Word. I knew this was no average message, but a defining moment in my life.

You know how it is—when you hear something so profound that it stays with you for a lifetime. Although I wrote out Ney's definition of faith in my notes, I didn't really need to, for I already had memorized the words. I've never forgotten them. She explained that every demonstration of faith in the Bible shows someone taking God at His Word. And where do we find His Word? In the Bible. I thought to myself, *If faith is taking God at His Word, then knowing God's Word is one of the most important goals I can have in my life.*

After listening to Ney's message at that conference, I determined that for the rest of my life I would know God's Word better than I knew magazines, newspapers, other books, or anything else. I would set aside many other activities to give God enough time to teach me in His Word. I wanted to be like that centurion and hear Jesus say, "Catherine has a great faith." And Ney taught me the secret that day— know God's Word and take God at His Word.

I could relate to Hannah Whitall Smith, who discovered the importance of God's Word in her life and cultivated this response: "It was no longer, 'How do I feel?' but always 'What does God say?'"[2] Devotion to God and His Word became the foundation of my dance with Him. And indeed, living in the Bible is the essential part of our dance, for God speaks in His Word, and we respond in faith by taking Him at His Word. Ours is a faith dance, one step of faith at a time.

What would you do if someone knocked at your door and said, "Jesus is coming to your house today"? That's just how it was for a woman named Martha who welcomed Jesus into her home in Bethany. Two miles outside of Jerusalem, just beyond the Mount of Olives, was the small village of Bethany, a regular stop for Jesus in His travels. He stayed more than once with His friends Mary, Martha, and Lazarus, whom He loved (John 11:5).

On this day Jesus arrived with all of His disciples, a large enough group to challenge anyone wanting to provide an inviting home and warm hospitality. I can imagine Martha thinking, *There is so much I must do to get dinner ready. Prepare the food. Prepare the table. Prepare the drinks. Prepare. Prepare. Prepare.* All she could think of was the work she had to do. Then a new thought came to her: *I need help! Why can't Mary help me? I'm here all alone serving all these people. It's not fair.* She looked, and there was Mary, seated at the Lord's feet and listening to His word. Maybe she even thought, *I'd like to be sitting down listening along with everyone else.* The more Martha thought about it all, the more upset she became.

I love thinking about this scenario because I can relate to Mary and I can relate to Martha. Without a doubt, I am both women. Here I see the beauty of Jesus in action with His dancers Mary and Martha. But on this occasion, one is dancing, and the other has either stopped dancing or perhaps has not yet started. And wherever we are in the dance, we need to remember that Jesus always wants us in the dance with Him. I love knowing that Jesus was aware of where Mary was, but He was also completely aware of Martha there in the kitchen, serving and making preparations. Martha thought she was alone, but she was not, for Jesus knew what she was thinking and what was in her heart.

She came to Jesus and said, "Lord, do You not care that my sister has left me to do all the serving alone? Then tell her to help me" (Luke 10:40). I'm certain that Martha thought Jesus would agree with her because the occasion clearly called for preparations and service, and four hands were surely much better than two. But Jesus never responds as we might imagine because God's thoughts and ways are higher than our thoughts and ways (Isaiah 55:8-9).

I think about her words, "Do you not care?" How many times have I said that to the Lord? *Lord, don't You care about all I have to do right now?* I've said those words when I'm in a hurry and stuck in rush-hour traffic. I've said those words when working until midnight on a project. I've said those words when everything goes wrong at once in my life. Here's the thing—I know He cares. But when I lose focus and sit down, refusing to dance, I lose sight of what I know to be true about God. But Jesus never stops inviting me to dance with Him, just as He never stopped reaching out to Martha.

Jesus focused all His attention on Martha and began by saying her name: "Martha, Martha." Just the repetition of her name is endearing and demonstrates His love for her. Then He said, "You are worried and bothered about so many things; but only one thing is necessary, for Mary has chosen the good part, which shall not be taken away from her." Jesus contrasts the actions of Martha and Mary, their choices, their focus, and their priorities. Martha was worried and bothered. Mary was sitting at Jesus' feet. Martha had chosen the wrong thing, and Mary had chosen the "good part," which would last forever. Martha was focused on many things, and Mary was focused on one thing. Martha focused on things that were not necessary. Mary focused on the one thing that was necessary.

Here is the bottom line. Mary was dancing, and Martha was not, at least not at that moment. I believe Martha could have danced, even in the kitchen. Jesus didn't say she shouldn't be serving. He said the error was becoming distracted, worried, and bothered in the service. Sometimes we are called to sit, and sometimes we are called to serve. Either way we can dance.

I think it's important to note the position of Mary, seated there at the feet of Jesus, listening to His word. Her action is quite radical for the day. Only disciples sat at the feet of their teachers. She had taken the position of a disciple, truly engaging in the dance with her Lord, following His lead in her life.

We know Martha did not make the right choice because Jesus told her so. She was looking at the many things instead of focusing on Jesus, the one thing, even in her service. And is not our focus often in the wrong place? Someone else may be doing what we would like to be doing while we are not living the life we hoped for or dreamed of. Jesus may have led us in an unusual direction that required us to let go of one vocation in order to say yes and follow His lead. Friend, know this—whether you are sitting like Mary or serving like Martha, you can always dance with Jesus and listen to His word.

I truly can relate to Martha, so distracted that all I can hear are my own worries and agitation. Had Martha leaned in and danced, even in her service she could have heard the word of the Lord. I doubt that the house was so large that she could not have interacted with Jesus and listened to Him teach. In fact, she did engage in conversation with Him about Mary's actions.

We can learn so much from Martha and Mary. Martha helps me understand that service can become distracting and can lead to agitation and worry, keeping me from dancing with the Lord. Mary helps me understand that my devotion to Jesus, sitting at His feet and listening to His Word, is at the heart of my dance with Him.

I walked into the cafeteria at Arizona State University. Grabbing some coffee, I made my way to a secluded table that would become my sanctuary for some of the most intimate times of my dance with the Lord for the next two years. I put my backpack down on a chair, sat down, and pulled out my Bible. *Now what? Where do I begin? I know I'm supposed to have that thing called a quiet time, but what am I supposed to actually do?*

I looked across the aisle, and two tables away, I noticed a girl sitting there with her Bible, a notebook, and another book. *Hmm...She seems to know what she's doing.* So I just sat and watched this girl. I watched her read in her Bible and then write in her notebook. After a while, I saw her reading the other book. As she was putting all her materials in her backpack, she noticed me watching. Smiling, she walked over and said, "Hi. I'm Denny."

"Hi. I'm Catherine. I noticed you reading your Bible. Do you do this every morning?"

"Yes, it's my quiet time."

Then I asked a monumental and life-changing question: "Denny, what exactly do you do in your quiet time?"

I smile now to think of it. I didn't know that one day I would lead Quiet Time Ministries, traveling and teaching others how to have a quiet time with the Lord. At that moment, I was teachable and hungry to learn, like a sponge soaking up every drop of water. Denny shared her quiet time with me. She said, "I begin reading in the Bible and writing my thoughts in my journal. Then I like to read through a book. Right now I'm reading a book by Ann Kiemel."

That's enough to get me started. I immediately bought a notebook for my quiet time and got the Ann Kiemel book she was reading. I figured if it was good enough for her quiet time, it was good enough for mine.

The next day, I went to the same table in the cafeteria, but I was much more confident in my quiet time. I decided I would read through the Gospel of Mark one chapter at a time. I began by writing some of my thoughts about my life at college in my notebook. I found that the writing slowed my mind down, allowing me to think more deeply about spiritual truth. I read a chapter in the Bible. Then I started reading my Ann Kiemel book. I wrote some more thoughts in my notebook. The time went much more quickly than I could imagine. I looked over at my friend Denny. *Lord, I'm so thankful for Denny teaching me about quiet time.*

But that was only the beginning. Leann, one of the staff members of Campus Crusade, began to disciple me, showing me many positions and moves in the dance. I asked her all kinds of questions about my dance with the Lord. "How do I study the Bible? How do I spend time with the Lord? How do I share my faith?" Leann poured her life into mine and taught me all about what it means to be a Christian. I attended conferences with Leann and some of the other girls. I was always watching what Leann did. She had a little blue Bible she took everywhere with her. I watched her sit alone with the Lord and just live in that Bible.

Over the years I made a habit of asking everyone I met, "What do you do in your quiet time?" I spent hours in Christian bookstores, learning how to use Bible study tools so I could listen better to God in His Word. I've made a point to develop and deepen my life of devotion with one goal in mind—to dance with the Lord, to know Him intimately and love Him wholeheartedly.

Here is what I've learned after many years of dancing with the Lord. A woman with a heart that dances has a heart of devotion to God and prioritizes her time alone with Him. Your quiet time alone with God is at the heart of your dance with Him. In your quiet time, you engage in the most precious parts of your dance—communion, prayer, contemplation of what God says in His Word, surrender, resolve, and commitment. In your quiet time, God will share the secrets of His heart with you from His love letter, the Bible. Such secrets are not hidden, but simply undiscovered until we open the pages of God's Word. In fact, every time you grab your Bible, imagine His standing invitation to dance with Him all across the pages of His Word. Every day is a new adventure, for God speaks His Word with purpose into your life (see Isaiah 55:10-11).

We know that "the word of God is living and active and sharper than any two-edged sword" and is "able to judge the thoughts and intentions of the heart" (Hebrews 4:12). In God's Word, He will teach you how to dance and will lead you in new steps along the way. All these aspects of the dance occur when you spend time alone with your Lord. If you would dance with the Lord and enjoy the intimate communion that other great dancers throughout the history of the church have known, be sure to pay much attention to your quiet time with Him.

Set aside a time each day to dance with your Lord in your quiet time. I am thankful for my internal alarm clock that wakes me up early every morning. Not everyone has that luxury, so you might have to get a good alarm clock. In fact, morning might not be the best time for you to meet alone with God. Evening may be better for you. Schedule your time with the Lord and hold that time more sacred than anything else you do in the day. Don't be afraid to say no to some good things in your life in order to say yes to the best—time with your Lord.

Then find a quiet place to dance with your Lord in quiet time.

Andrew Murray encourages us to choose a fixed spot where we can meet with Him daily. He says, "The inner chamber, that solitary place, is Jesus' schoolroom. That spot can be anywhere. It can even change from day to day if we're traveling. But that secret place must be somewhere with quiet time for the pupil to place himself in the Master's presence."[3]

Organize all your quiet time materials in your quiet place. I like to use a basket for my *Quiet Time Notebook*, Bible, devotionals, books, hymnbook, and other resources. Some use a briefcase, and others, a backpack. I've found that keeping all my quiet time materials in one place helps me remain faithful to dance in quiet time with my Lord.

Finally, you need a plan for your dance in quiet time. I like to use the PRAYER quiet time plan:

Prepare Your Heart
Read and Study God's Word
Adore God in Prayer
Yield Yourself to God
Enjoy His Presence
Rest in His Love.[4]

I find this plan helps me remember all the ways to dance in quiet time.

We need to cultivate devotion in our dance because the busyness of our culture is eating us alive. The number of burnout casualties in the church should lead us to concern and caution. Can we think of even one moment when we don't have something we need to do? I live in an area of the United States that attracts a lot of retired people. I am constantly amazed at how busy retired people are—sometimes busier than those who work in full-time jobs.

Interestingly, when Jesus told Martha she was "worried and bothered about so many things," He was actually telling her that she was worried about and busy with many things. That's the meaning behind the word *bothered*. Jesus was pointing out to Martha and to us the danger of busyness at the expense of devotion in the dance. When we are so busy that we lose the soothing refreshment of quiet and solitude with our Lord, and when we no longer think deeply about anything, we are too busy. Never fear; Jesus will continue to initiate in your dance with Him. He is faithful and will have us for His own. Kay Arthur talks about her focus on receiving God's Word:

> When I've guarded the time that leads to intimacy with the Lord, when I'm deeply rooted in the Word and my prayer life is thriving, I am less prone to feel that my own spiritual journey is inferior or lacking just because someone else experiences God differently than I. Without a firm foundation of Scripture and prayer, I know that I, like others, can fall prey to every new trend that guarantees true spirituality. And before long, instead of listening to God, I'm listening to whoever comes along claiming to have found what I may have been missing.[5]

I am constantly reexamining my schedule and changing it around to guard my quiet time with the Lord. I want to dance with Him.

Your dance in your quiet time occurs in many different contexts of life, and it won't always look the same from season to season. I often think of Susannah Wesley (with her 19 children) standing in the middle of her kitchen and throwing her apron over her head for some solitude in her quiet time. Now there's a woman who was determined to dance with the Lord. And your devotion in your dance with the Lord will require determination, persistence, and intention. But the result is worth it—you will dance.

Always remember that your devotion to the Lord is a dance with Him, not an academic acquiring of facts. It's a relationship, a communion with your Lord. Carole Mayhall talks about a time early in her marriage when her spiritual life was stagnant. Her life was all about "going through the motions" and "dishes, dust, and diapers."[6] Her husband began discipleship meetings with a friend and started memorizing Scripture. She noticed a significant change in his behavior toward her. He was more loving and patient, applying the Scripture he was memorizing to every circumstance in his life.

One day in particular, his love was so evident to her that she became overwhelmed with her own lack in her relationship with God. She describes her defining moment this way: "I knew if I didn't let God do something deep and significant in my life, soon Jack and I would be worlds apart." She began learning about the spiritual life from her husband. But her quiet time with the Lord was what revolutionized her life.

> What made the greatest difference in opening up God's riches and making my faith authentic was examining my time alone with God…I hadn't been *meeting God*. I had been meeting a habit…Now when I study the Bible and pray, I come before the Lord expecting that He will have something to teach me. I spend more time listening for His voice instead of getting caught up in my own meaningless words.

One woman wrote in a Quiet Time Bible study that she is currently experiencing a revolution of love in her heart. She suddenly realized her main goal in life of knowing God. She described it this way:

> I've always considered my life goal to be things like this: being a godly woman, being a good wife, raising godly children. All very worthy things. But this is what I learned this week: my (our!) overarching goal should be that of knowing God. Intimately, radically, amazingly knowing God. And if we do that, all the other things I mentioned? They will flow out of that. Throughout Scripture we see example after example of people who just want to know God more—Moses, David, Hosea, Zaccheus, Paul, and more. They made getting to know

God better their goal in life, more important than any other task. For years, basically as long as I've been a Christian, I've always wanted to have a regular, meaningful devotional life. "Quiet time," as it's known to many. But my motivation was completely wrong. I thought that if I were really a "good Christian" I'd be having a regular quiet time. That is probably true, but it's just a slightly skewed perspective. I have been so in love with the Word this week because I have come to see that I want to *know* God. Not just check off a box in my schedule somewhere that says, "Have quiet time." No, the motivation isn't just to become a better Christian. It's to get to know Him. To fall deeply in love with God. To understand His heart. It's a call to, as Catherine Martin would put it, *radical intimacy.*[7]

I love what this young woman has discovered, for it is one of the great secrets of a magnificent dance with the Lord in life.

One of the most important aspects of ballet is learning to spot—focusing your eyes on a particular spot in the room and keeping your eyes on it to the very last second before you pirouette on pointes or demi-pointes. This same kind of focus is essential in our devotion in the dance—our eyes are always on our dance Partner, the Lord. When we open our Bible and read His Word, we listen for what He has to say to us. When we pray, we are talking with Him. That's the dance—intimate communion, a sharing of His heart and yours.

But devotion in the dance includes discipline as we practice our moves and always maintain our focus on our Partner. If we don't practice, we lose the essentials in our dance. If I never open my Bible, I can't expect to hear what God has to say to me, for He speaks in His Word. If I never talk with Him, I can't expect to experience that intimate communion He promises. There's the practice, the discipline. When you lose the devotion of your dance, you need to step back into the discipline, the practice of quiet time. Begin again with a time, a place, and a plan.

In my first year of college, I had the opportunity to attend gymnastics practice with a coach who was involved in the Olympics. We spent four hours practicing the first day of gymnastics class. She had me doing back handsprings and backflips all the way down the mat, something I'd never done before. What an exhilarating day! The next day when I woke up, I thought, *I have never been in so much pain before.* My legs hurt so much I couldn't walk down any stairs for a week!

Muscles that haven't been used for a long time will hurt when you begin using them again. The same is true in your life of devotion. Devotion is exercise for your heart, and you will find with time that you will dance with greater ease and agility. At first, you may feel awkward and unsure as you draw near to your Lord in the dance. But you can trust Jesus to lead you in your devotional time alone with Him. And you will dance.

My quiet time is my favorite part of my dance with the Lord. I love nothing more than gathering my quiet time materials and sitting alone with Him. I always look forward to the special moments He and I share alone together. I often think about the day when I will step from time into eternity. I want to look into eyes that are familiar, and I want to connect with a knowing smile of shared experience. I want to be able to say to Jesus, "I so loved our dance together. What incredible moments we had. Thank You for inviting me and for leading me every step of the way." What a moment that will be!

7

Embrace

W hen I began ballet lessons, I soon discovered how difficult and intense ballet was. When I watched a ballet performance on television or at the theater, the ballerinas danced so gracefully and effortlessly, I thought learning their moves would be easy. But each class offered new challenges for me, and the positions and moves were not easily acquired. I was determined, but I needed practice, and my body and muscles needed to mature. After all, I was only six years old.

In the back of my mind was one big dream related to ballet— I wanted to dance on toe shoes, or pointes. Impatient, I would ask, "When can I have toe shoes?"

"Not yet," my teacher would reply. I kept asking and always received the same response. When she finally realized that like most children, I was going to keep asking until I got what I wanted, she said, "It's going to be *many years* before you will have those shoes you want so much. You must be ready to dance on pointe, and you are not ready yet."

Ballet requires students to surrender to and trust in the wisdom and expertise of their instructors. One man tells the story of his 12-year-old daughter, Amanda, who seemed to outshine all the others in her ballet class. Her father was afraid that if she didn't advance to the next dance level, she might lose interest. So the parents set up a meeting with the head of the dance studio. They pointed out their daughter's wonderful stage presence and graceful movement. The head of the dance studio nodded his head and agreed. But he said he did not think she should be moved ahead.

"Yes, she moves well and presents herself beautifully, but that is not the discipline of ballet. What we teach is the dancer's position at the start of each move and at the end of each move. How she gets from point A to point B is up to her individuality, her imagination, and her artistry. Amanda needs to improve her focus, her concentration, and the position of her head and eyes before and after moves. That is what she must learn to proceed to the next level."

Discipline is not all that is necessary to move to the stage of dancing on pointe. Other considerations include strength, length of study, age, bone development, ankle and foot anatomy, weight, and attitude. So when the teacher says, "Not yet," she often has good reasons and is making a wise decision. Students must trust their teachers and surrender to their ways.

Finally the day came when Arnora, my ballet instructor, said, "It's time to fit you with pointe shoes." I was thrilled. Little did I know this would be a new surrender and trust for me in ballet. I had to remove my old shoes to put on the new. And then, once I put on those long-awaited toe shoes, I was very disappointed. Wearing them was nothing like what I expected. Those beautiful pink shoes with ribbons laced around my ankles felt strange and difficult to move in at first.

And so began my pointe work in ballet school. I faced the barre and practiced rolling up onto pointe slowly and then rolling back down again. I was excited to be on toe shoes, but I was discouraged at how slow-going and rigorous the training was. I wanted to dance across the stage like Margot Fonteyn right away, but first I had to enter a new level of surrender and trust, persist in the practice and learning, and embrace this new stage in my ballet training.

— ✳ —

Every day of our lives requires a new surrender and trust if we would lean into the embrace of Jesus and follow His lead in our dance with Him. Even if we are skilled in this dance with our Lord, He will lead us in new directions that require new levels of surrender. Such was the case in the lives of Mary and Martha of Bethany. We know they danced with the Lord. Mary's dance with Jesus is celebrated in more than one place in Scripture. But now her dance with Him was about to be taken deeper—would she embrace Him in the midst of a great loss when He did not act as she had expected or hoped He would?

Martha and Mary were experiencing the greatest crisis of their lives. Their brother Lazarus was gravely ill, so the two sisters sent word to Jesus. "Lord, behold, he whom You love is sick." When Jesus received their message He said, "This sickness is not to end in death" (John 11:4). Here is where the story becomes strange and interesting at the same time. Jesus did not rush to help Lazarus. He never displayed one ounce of worry or fear, and He never questioned what was going to happen to Lazarus. He was so seemingly indifferent that He stayed where He was for two more days. He seemed to be on a schedule that only He knew and that was excruciatingly slow for Mary and Martha. Two days must have seemed like two years or even two decades to them.

But eventually, finally, He said to His disciples, "Let us go to Judea again." And then He broke the news to everyone traveling with Him. "Lazarus is dead." But He continued, "I am glad for your sakes that I was not there, so that you may believe; but let us go to him." Here we clearly see at least one purpose for His delay—He was testing and strengthening the disciples' faith.

As Jesus approached Bethany, the news of His coming reached Mary and Martha. If you had never read the story, which sister would you guess ran to meet Him, Mary or Martha? Your first guess may be Mary, the one whose dance is celebrated so graphically in the Bible. But actually, Martha was the one who jumped up and ran to meet Jesus. I find this so very interesting and also comforting.

Mary was probably experiencing a huge crisis of surrender and trust. She knew that if Jesus had come more quickly, He could have saved Lazarus. I think Mary was so grief-stricken that perhaps her emotions bordered on despair and disillusionment. He could have saved her brother, and yet He didn't. Her devastated emotional state is comforting to me because I can know that regardless of how far along in the dance I may be, I too may have times of crisis and disappointment when my Lord does not always lead in the way I expect. Even then, I can still dance with Him.

Martha and Mary were both suffering the tragic loss of their precious brother, Lazarus. But something had entered Martha's mind that perhaps had not occurred to Mary. When Martha met Jesus, she said, "Lord, if You had been here, my brother would not have died." But Martha did not stop there. She continued, "Even now I know that whatever You ask of God, God will give You." Oh, I love this statement! Martha was surrendered, trusting and leaning into the embrace of Jesus in her dance with Him. She knew that even though she did not understand why Lazarus died, Jesus was not worried, and He must have known something that she didn't know.

I love Martha's words "Even now." She knew she could always have hope when Jesus was involved. He may not do what we desire, but He has a plan and a purpose even in our most devastating losses. Our emotions and grief in our losses may not yet have caught up with what we know to be true. Even so, may we, like Martha, with hearts filled with hope, run to Jesus, lean in to His embrace, and dance, trusting Him to lead in our lives.

Martha's actions were rewarded with an intimate revelation from Jesus about who He was and what He was going to do. And when we dance with Jesus in our deepest sufferings, yielding to a new level of surrender and trust, we are often given the greatest views of His character and His ways. He does indeed turn our mourning into dancing. In Martha's case, she learned that Jesus would raise Lazarus from the dead. Jesus said to her, "Your brother will rise again."

But Jesus did not stop there with His words. He continued by revealing one of the greatest promises any person can ever have—the promise of eternal life. "I am the resurrection and the life; he who believes in Me will live even if he dies." What blessing came to Martha in her surrender to Jesus! Jesus then brought Martha to a marvelous confession of faith. "Everyone who lives and believes in Me will never die. Do you believe this?"

Martha responded, "Yes Lord; I have believed that you are the Christ, the Son of God, even He who comes into the world." The Lord brought Martha to a deep faith and trust in Him in the midst of a tragic loss. And that is what the Lord often does in our own lives when we experience a grievous loss. He will bring us into the company of His great promises and ask, "Do you believe this?" What a dance Jesus and Martha experienced in that brief meeting prior to His arrival in Bethany at the tomb of Lazarus.

And now Jesus was going to reach out to His precious Mary, the dancer who had chosen what could never be taken from her. He knew what she was thinking and feeling. He sent Martha to Mary with a secret message: "The Teacher is here and is calling for you." How would Mary respond in her grief and loss? Jesus knew how she would respond, for He knew she was His dance partner—she had a heart that dances. When she heard His message, she immediately responded. It was what she needed—a word from Him.

She got up quickly and ran to Him. "Lord, if You had been here, my brother would not have died." She fell at His feet weeping. And that's what dancers sometimes do—weep uncontrollably when they are broken and crushed in spirit. But Jesus, the Lover of our souls, shares even the depth of our emotion when we dance with Him.

How did Jesus respond to His Mary? His response is contained in two words that mean everything to you and me: "Jesus wept." Tears flowed down His face from the emotion He felt in His heart. When you weep, Jesus weeps with you. And together you enter into the dance of tears. The dance of tears with Jesus is a precious intimacy He shares only with those who have known deep suffering. In the dance of tears,

Jesus shares your pain. He carries your deep sorrows in His everlasting arms. And He ultimately turns your mourning into dancing. He revives and saves your crushed spirit. What a blessed comfort in our deepest darkness to know the One who shares the depth of every pain and loss, every joy and gladness. Jesus. He is the One.

Now Jesus was compelled to action. The time had come for His great and mighty work for all to see, even those of us in this generation. Jesus perfectly timed every move—He is never early or late, but right on time. "Jesus, again being deeply moved within, came to the tomb...Jesus said, 'Remove the stone.'"

Martha protested, knowing that her brother had been dead four days and the smell of decomposition would be overwhelming. Jesus reminded her of what He had told her He would do. "Did I not say to you that if you believe, you will see the glory of God?" So they removed the stone.

Now we are given just a glimpse into the eternal dance of triune God. Jesus raised His eyes and said, "Father, I thank You that You have heard Me."

After He prayed to His Father, He cried out with a loud voice, "Lazarus, come forth." Imagine being there, standing in anticipation, watching the opening of the cave. What would happen? Would anything in fact happen? Imagine the drama of watching a man, completely bound in burial linens, walk out of that cave alive and well. I wonder if anyone fainted. I would have been jumping up and down with tears of joy rolling down my face. I would have been shouting, "God, You are amazing!" Truly, that day, Jesus turned mourning into dancing.

As I pulled into the church parking lot, my thoughts were hundreds of miles away. I was worried about my mother. Again. I was frustrated because I could not control her advancing stages of multiple sclerosis. I'm a doer and a fixer, but this time, things just were not turning out as I planned. I sat there with my car engine still on, the air conditioner blowing full blast because of the 100-degree heat. I was paralyzed with worry. The more I thought, the deeper my worry. Then I started doing what I often do in those times. I pulled out my bag of worries.

Will my niece Kayla know and trust Jesus? Will my brother's hand get better? Time is moving fast. I'm not as young as I once was or as old as I'm going to be. Why can't I fit into my favorite white pants anymore? When am I going to cut the carbs more and increase the protein? My bag of worries seemed to be getting bigger. As I sat in the car that day, I realized that I have serious issues of trust. *That's it. I need to trust in God more than anything else.*

That day marked a new level of surrender for me. *Lord, I confess to You that I don't seem to trust You in any area of my life. But I want Your way more than mine. I need to trust You more.* The Lord was calling me to surrender, lean in, embrace Him, and learn to trust Him in the dance. Surrender was necessary if I was to learn something new from my Lord. And I was ready to learn because I was tired of the worry and stressful anxiety. From that day on, I began to study trust in earnest. I learned that trust is Total Reliance Under Stress and Trial. I also learned that I couldn't dance very well if I didn't trust my eternal dance Partner.

This is when I began to understand the great value of devotion to the dance and how it leads me to surrender. The Lord uses our quiet time together to show me what I need to learn and apply in my life. I must make decisions and resolves from the truths I've seen in God's Word. Will I respond to His lead as He shows me what I need to learn, know, and live out in my life? My response always requires surrender as I say to Him, *Lord, I want Your way, not my own.* Always I need to let go of my ways to say yes to His way. Sometimes saying yes is easy. Other times, I seem to wrestle, not wanting to let go of what seems safe to me.

The Lord helped me learn to trust Him by leading me to a very powerful portion of Scripture one day. In Isaiah 7, King Ahaz of Judah heard some news that frightened him—the kings of Syria and

Israel were forming an alliance and threatening to come against him and his people. This news propelled King Ahaz and the people into a panic attack. They were so afraid of what might happen that they "trembled with fear, like trees shaking in a storm" (Isaiah 7:2 NLT). Have you ever felt like a tree shaking in a storm? Well, maybe you haven't, but I surely have! In fact, sometimes I think I have the gift of fear and worry because those emotions come over me so quickly and easily when crises strike in my life.

God sent Isaiah to King Ahaz with a message. This message is one for the ages, and we need to remember it every single time we are tempted not to trust God in our situation. The Lord said to Isaiah, "Tell him to stop worrying. Tell him he doesn't need to fear" (Isaiah 7:4 NLT). I love the fact that God confronted Ahaz about his response to the threat in his life.

Worry and fear are two giants, but we can overcome them with the power of God's Word and His Holy Spirit. The question is, will we surrender to fear and worry, or will we surrender to the truth of God and His Word? God used this account in Isaiah to ask me that question. He taught me that embracing Him in the dance will require a true surrender to Him and His Word, and the result will be trust.

God continued with Ahaz by revealing that the two kings aligned against him were really "burned-out embers" and that the threatened invasion would never take place. This is important to consider. Ahaz's fears and worries were based on threats. Nothing had actually happened. And is that not often the case with us? Our fears are very often based on what-ifs and if-onlys. God gave Ahaz a dose of reality to ward off his fears and worries. And then God told Ahaz what was lacking in his life: "Unless your faith is firm, I cannot make you stand firm" (Isaiah 7:9 NLT). When I read those words, I was shaken to the core of my being. I realized, *Catherine, you need to surrender in a new way in your dance with the Lord. He wants you to lay aside worry and fear and become firm in your faith. When you do, your dance with Him can go in the direction He desires.*

I was absolutely floored because I am known for a strong faith and faithfulness to the Lord. But He had struck at the core of something in my heart that only He saw, and now He was dealing with it. He was calling me to a new level of surrender. I had to lay aside this habit of embracing worry and fear when difficulty came my way. Only then could I trust the Lord to lead me in my dance with Him. In fact, I believe He was bringing me to this new level of surrender because of where He wanted to lead me in the dance in the days and months and years to come. It always comes down to His way or my way. And God made very clear to me that just as in the life of Ahaz, so in my life: My response was not to be based on fear or worry, but on a firm faith and trust in Him.

Nancy Leigh DeMoss speaks of cultivating a lifestyle of surrender in her book *Surrender: The Heart God Controls*. This lifestyle of surrender is necessary if we want to embrace our Lord and dance. When we surrender, we hand over the privilege of power and control, and we yield to God and His ways. As you dance with the Lord, could you be holding on to attitudes and actions that keep you from moving freely and fluidly with Him? Perhaps you are experiencing a dark night of the soul, a life change, or a great sadness that has taken you, like Mary, into the dance of tears. Perhaps you are afraid to lean in to the Lord's embrace because of the pain you have endured. Dear friend, you can trust your Lord as you surrender anew in your dance with Him.

Letting go of fear and worry was difficult for me. I somehow believed that if I continued to be afraid about what might happen or worried about what was happening, I was doing something to help the situation. In reality, I was actually holding on to the controls of my life. I guess I was thinking that if I exercised enough fear and worry, I could change my situation. I know it sounds ridiculous, and it is. But there you have it. I confess that at times I fail miserably. But the Lord still engages me in the dance.

Or perhaps fear and worry isn't your struggle. Maybe you have struggles with a difficult spouse or child, a job, your future or your past, or even an addiction of some kind. Maybe you wrestle with bitterness, anger, jealousy, or insecurity. Sometime in your dance, God will call you to a new level of surrender in the midst of your issues and in the heart of your difficulty. He pulls you into His embrace because He wants to dance with you in an intimate, vibrant, dynamic, life-changing, forever relationship. Nancy DeMoss describes surrender this way:

> The terms of our surrender to the Lord Jesus are non-negotiable and unconditional. What does He ask us to surrender? In a word, *everything.* Christian surrender means that we come to Him on His terms as the conquering General of our soul and simply say, "I surrender all." We lay down our arms, we hand over everything we have, everything we are, everything we hope to be.[1]

I've heard surrender described as taking a blank piece of paper (representing our life), signing it at the bottom, handing it to the Lord, and saying, "Lord, fill it in as You please."

A.W. Tozer speaks of our surrender as "irrevocable attachment" and says we "sink or swim, live or die, irrevocably attached in love and faith and devotion to Jesus Christ the Lord." Such a dancer, according to Tozer, is "facing only one direction." If she hears anything behind her, she can't turn around to see what's going on. She has stopped looking back. That's surrender into the blessed embrace of Jesus.

I am happy to say I eventually responded to the Lord's invitation and handed over my bag of worries. I admit that sometimes I try to grab it back, but He quickly reminds me that I need to leave it with Him. And truthfully, I've been set free from living in fear and worry about things, walking in a new confident trust. I have learned to lean in to the safe and secure embrace of Jesus and eagerly watch to see what He is going to do. And you too can lean in to your Lord's embrace and surrender to His control in the dance.

—※—

Quickly surrendering to the Lord is much easier for us if we are cultivating a humble heart. Humility encourages a lifestyle of surrender and empowers us to lean into the embrace of our Lord. Humility means we make a true estimate of ourselves and depend on God, realizing our own inadequacy and weakness apart from Him. Humility shares in the life of Jesus and focuses on His desires instead of our own.

Moses was known as the most humble man on the face of the earth (Numbers 12:3). When God spoke to Moses from the burning bush, He told Moses, "Remove your sandals from your feet, for the place on which you are standing is holy ground" (Exodus 3:5). Removing his shoes was a surrender of heart and an act of humility for Moses. And so it is for you. In humility you will learn to "remove your shoes" in surrender to your Lord. I like to think of those beautiful toe shoes hanging by their ribbons, waiting for me to remove the old shoes and replace them with the new. When we "remove our shoes," we humble ourselves under God's mighty hand. This is what Peter encourages us to do in times of difficulty or hardship (1 Peter 5:6).

The Lord began teaching me this humble surrender in a new way shortly after David and I married. I was so excited to be married, and in my mind, my new husband was perfect in every way. But sure enough, one morning after we had been married about six months, we had a disagreement. He left for work, and I sat in our bedroom, frustrated and upset. Tender in heart, I thought, *I'm right and he's wrong. I have a right to be angry.* For a few moments, all I could think about was avoiding any conflict. *Maybe I'll just drive away.*

And then I thought, *Well then, Catherine, just where do you think you're going to go?* The Lord started working in my heart and in my thoughts. As I came to my senses, I began submitting my heart and my thoughts to God. *I've made a commitment of marriage to my husband before the Lord. I wonder what He wants me to do.* I sat on the floor of the bedroom with my Bible open. The Lord led me to 1 Peter 5:6 and seemed to be saying, *Catherine, humble yourself under My mighty hand, that I may lift you up in due time.*

I soon realized that if I wanted to dance with the Lord, I couldn't demand my own rights. I needed to remove my shoes, lean in, surrender to the Lord, and then watch what He would do. I'm so glad I listened to the Lord. Within hours, the frustration I had felt melted away, and David and I resolved our conflict. And to top it off, he came home with fresh flowers and a warm embrace!

Isn't that what often happens when God leads us to a new level of surrender? Once we yield to Him, He leads us in our dance in ways that we had never even imagined, and we quickly forget what all the difficulty was about. That experience of surrender so many years ago was worthwhile indeed and taught me a valuable lesson in relationships. David and I just celebrated our twenty-seventh wedding anniversary, and I am privileged to be married to the most amazing and wonderful man in the world—the one who was God's choice and who is absolutely perfect for me.

Have you ever danced with the one you love? On a moonlit evening in Kona, Hawaii, David and I sat in an elegant restaurant. The window shutters were wide open to the warm night air, and from our table we could see the stars. My words of gratitude to David flowed easily. "Isn't it beautiful here? Honey, thank you for bringing me to dinner with you here tonight. I love being with you."

A band was playing romantic music in the background, but I barely heard it because I was totally focused on my husband. When the band began playing a song that's always been special to David and me, "My Funny Valentine," my husband, ever the romantic, stood, walked around the table to me, held out his hand, and asked, "Will you dance with me?" I looked into his loving eyes, grabbed his hand, and found myself swept onto the dance floor. There I was in my love's embrace, being led in the most wonderful dance. It was a moment etched in time for me.

And that's how it is when we truly lean in to the embrace of the Lord and dance—we will experience moments of delight and love with Him. So, my dear friend, step into a new level of surrender and trust, saying yes to whatever He asks of you, and you will be a woman with a heart that dances.

> i stand before Christ and the world.
> my heart shouts an affirmation:
> Jesus, i am a lowly servant woman.
> take me…all of me.
> add anything. take away anything.
> at any cost. with any price.
> make me Yours. completely…wholly.
> may i not be remembered for
> how i wear my hair
> or the shape of my face
> or the people i know
> or the crowds i've addressed.
> may i be known for loving You…
> for carrying a dream…
> for building bridges
> to the hurt and broken and lost in the world.
> make me what You would be if You lived
> in Person where i do.
> may everything accomplished through my simple life
> bring honor and glory to You.
> take my human failures and flaws,
> and use them to remind these who know me
> that only You are God.
> and i will always just be ann.
> amen
> amen.[2]

Ann Kiemel Anderson

Part 3

Lord, I Love to Dance with You

8

Steps

From her youth, Agrippina Yakovlevna Vaganova (1879–1951) sought excellence and precision in ballet, first as a dancer and later as an instructor. She was a brilliant dancer of the Maryinsky Theater and became famous as the "queen of variations" in ballets where leading roles were performed by such greats as Anna Pavlova and Tamara Karsavina. Extremely critical and demanding of herself, she became aware of her inadequate dance technique. She describes her feelings graphically and personally: "It was obvious I was not progressing. And that was a terrible thing to realize. So then, I started to feel pangs of dissatisfaction both with myself and with the old system of teaching."[1]

Following her retirement from dancing ballet on the stage, she became consumed with finding effective means of training classical ballerinas. Her book, *Basic Principles of Classical Ballet,* is filled with exercises and descriptions of individual steps and their combinations. Many dance teachers believe it should be in every dancer's library.

Movements in ballet are combinations of a myriad of individual steps. These steps are derived from the basic positions every beginning dancer learns at the barre. Similarly, our dance of steps and movements with the Lord is guided and directed by the Lord Himself. He is infinitely creative and leads us through unlimited variations of steps in the dance. We have a guidebook, the Bible, helping us learn the basic moves in our dance. And living in us is the Holy Spirit, who teaches us how to move one step at a time.

My husband and I left our cab at the base of San Pietro in Vincoli. When I saw how many steps I had to climb, I wanted to give up and go somewhere else. But I found if I just took one step after another, I eventually made it to the top. Walking into this church in Rome, I soon saw my reward for the long ascent—the intricate sculpture of Moses by Michelangelo. I told my husband, "Honey, thank you for insisting we come here. I would have been sad to miss this amazing piece of art." Most people never see the statue of Moses because the small chapel housing this magnificent work is tucked away near the Roman Coliseum. It's not even listed in some of the Rome guidebooks. But I had a great tour guide (my husband), so I saw all the best sights on our trip throughout Italy.

In the same way that all those steps brought a great reward for me in Rome, so too, following the Lord's lead through all the difficult and easy steps results in a great treasure and leads us in the direction God has planned for our life.

Every journey involves steps that take you from one place to another. Sometimes they lead from a low place to one much higher above you. Just look at the steps the Egyptians used to build the pyramids, which sometimes loom 138 meters high. Regardless of the height or the difficulty, when you take the appropriate steps, you make progress toward your destination.

Many years ago, my mother took my brother and me on the trip of all trips. She went to the American Automobile Association and planned our journey. One of the highlights of any trip planned by AAA is the TripTik, a free tour guide. The TripTik offers page-by-page directions for every destination of your trip. The AAA travel agent highlights your route on every page so you never have to wonder what road to take. Imagine my mother with two young children traveling from the Southwest to Montreal, from there to Niagara Falls, and on to Washington DC.

When I think of her planning that trip all by herself, I want to give her a standing ovation for her courage. At the time, I expected it of her. But now, I realize just how gutsy that was for her. But the Trip-Tik boosted her confidence to venture out into the unknown with her two eager and excited children. We reached each destination on our trip and arrived back home safe and sound. I still treasure many memories of that wonderful vacation.

The Lord has given you the best TripTiks for your journey—the Word of God and the Holy Spirit. Those who follow the Lord, listening to His Word and keeping in step with the Holy Spirit, will always arrive at their destination. Your dance with the Lord becomes a progression of steps leading to spiritual growth and maturity. Your dance is uniquely guided by God's plan and purpose, and the progression of steps will reflect the unique story He intends to tell in and through your life.

The time had finally arrived for Jesus to fulfill His purpose in leaving the palace of heaven and coming to earth in the incarnation. He was on a divine timetable, with the clock ticking off the minutes and hours until Passover. Only six days remained until His arrest, the mockery of a trial, and His crucifixion. He knew what was ahead, but most of His disciples did not. But at least one person seemed to sense what was about to happen.

Mary of Bethany had listened more carefully to Jesus than most of His followers. She had sat at His feet, soaking in His teaching. And now she was about to share in a meal with Him that promised to be a time of celebration. Perhaps Mary was thinking, *I can hardly believe*

*my brother, Lazarus, is alive! Tonight should be a joyous time. And yet I
sense something different in Jesus—perhaps a solemnity, a soberness, and
a resolute determination to travel a very difficult road.*

Mary loved Jesus with all her heart. Oh, how they had danced.
And she had grown in her spiritual journey with the One she knew to
be the Christ. Who knows the progression of thought that led her to
take a new step in her own dance with the Lord? Maybe she thought,
*I want to minister to my Lord. Something extravagant. What can I do to
bless Him beyond measure, to worship Him as my Lord in a unique way?*
She may have premeditated this outrageous act of love before Jesus
came to supper that night, procuring the perfume so she could carry
out her idea. However the plan came about, Mary knew her moment
had come. Perhaps she took a strange step for a woman, but she was
motivated to action from deep within her heart. She took a pound
of spikenard, a perfume costing a year's wage for a laborer, and knelt
down by the feet of her reclining Lord. She poured the perfume on
His feet, wiping them with her hair. In attending to Jesus' feet, she was
taking the place normally reserved for slaves. But she didn't care. Her
love, humility, and devotion compelled her to extravagant love. The
house was filled with the fragrance of the perfume Mary had chosen
to anoint the feet of her Lord.

Judas Iscariot, one of Jesus' disciples, was also at dinner that night,
but he had something else on his mind. He was a thief. He interpreted
Mary's action as a complete waste. He said, "Why was this perfume not
sold for three hundred denarii and given to poor people?" Of course,
Judas was not truly concerned for the poor. Again we see a contrast
between those who dance and those who don't. Judas clearly ran his
own life and was intending to betray Jesus.

But Mary danced, and Jesus knew it. Jesus revealed that Mary's
action was an important part of His plan and purpose; He affirmed
her step in the dance she enjoyed with Him in life. He interpreted her
action as a significant part of His Passion—she was anointing Him
for burial. He said, "Let her alone, so that she may keep it for the day

of My burial. For you always have the poor with you, but you do not always have Me" (John 12:7-8). Clearly Jesus was thinking about His impending suffering, death, and burial. Mary seems to have had a sense of the horror that was to come. Jesus welcomed her act of devotion and applauded the step she took in their dance together.

When I accepted Jesus' invitation to dance, I had no idea what was ahead for me. I was just excited about my new adventure with Him. I didn't know about the program of growth and maturity He had custom-designed for me. I didn't know that some of the steps He had in mind for me would be unusual and sometimes even painful. And perhaps some of your steps in the dance have been different from what you expected. But you can be sure that as you dance with the Lord, you will grow and mature through a journey of steps that the Lord has custom-designed just for you.

The Lord began my journey by teaching me about faith, and my "dance instructor" was Ney Bailey. I learned that faith is taking God at His Word, so I realized the importance of the Bible for my life. Then I learned that we walk by faith, not sight (2 Corinthians 5:7). In other words, every step in our dance is a step of faith.

We might think of the Bible as a book of steps. When the Lord, through the indwelling Holy Spirit, teaches us a truth from His Book, we respond in faith and live it out in our lives. Step by step, in faith, we move from one place to another. This happens both internally, as we mature and grow, and outwardly, as our Lord leads us in our daily decisions. David knew this when he said, "The LORD directs the steps of the godly. He delights in every detail of their lives. Though they stumble, they will never fall, for the LORD holds them by the hand" (Psalm 37:23 NLT).

I wish I could say that God's plan for our dance and the steps He lays out for us are eminently clear, like maps in our brains. But truthfully, almost every big step in my life has started out as either a happy surprise or a disappointment, and I would not initially have chosen many of them for myself. I want to share some secrets I've discovered—lessons turned upside down—that have helped me follow the Lord's lead and take the next step in my dance.

I almost stumbled early on as God directed my steps in an unusual direction that I misunderstood. As I anticipated graduating from college, I faced the uncertainty of my future. I knew God had a plan for me, but I didn't know what it was. Two choices stood out in my mind. I could become a staff member with Campus Crusade and disciple women on a campus somewhere in the United States, or I could accept a family friend's gift of free tuition to Moody Bible Institute.

You would think the Moody option was an obvious yes, but I felt unsure. I thought, *If I go on staff with Campus Crusade, I'll be able to share my faith and disciple women immediately. If I attend Moody Bible Institute, I'll spend more years studying in a library.* Riding the bus home one day from school I read in Ephesians 5:16 that I needed to make the most of my time because the days are evil. I continued reading, "So then do not be foolish, but understand what the will of the Lord is." I knew what the Lord wanted me to do: Go on staff with Campus Crusade.

Knowing my next step, I responded in faith and said, *Yes, Lord, I'll go.* But I said yes with all kinds of strings attached—I was going to disciple women on a campus somewhere. I had lots of plans for the next two years of my life. But God had something else in mind for our dance—Campus Crusade assigned me to be a secretary for Josh McDowell. *Whoa—wait a minute. A secretary? That's not what I had planned.*

Devastated, I decided to cancel my application to Campus Crusade. Then I opened my Bible in my quiet time and read a verse from the Lord. Once again, He guided my steps. I read, "The mind of man plans his way, but the LORD directs his steps" (Proverbs 16:9). *Okay, Lord, You seem to be showing me that Your ways will sometimes take me in unusual directions. Yet I can still count on You to direct my steps. Even in the placement with Josh McDowell Ministries, I can trust that You are directing my steps.* So I leaned in and said yes to the Lord, keeping in step with His plan. I'm so glad I bravely took that step because those four years were essential in preparing me for future ministry.

This lesson of God's guidance was one of the first ones the Lord began teaching me in my dance with Him, and it was not easy for me to accept. I still wrestle with the Lord's leading sometimes when He wants to go one direction and I very much want to go another. Perhaps you can relate to my struggle with wanting something so much and yet wanting what God wants even more. You've probably discovered, as I have, that sometimes our desires match God's direction for us, but sometimes they don't.

I learned to leave room for God's plans in my own desires and dreams because His ways are higher than my ways (Isaiah 55:9). I am still learning this secret in new ways because God continues to surprise me with ideas and plans my small mind has not yet even begun to entertain. And so, as I dance with the Lord, I try to hold my ideas, dreams, desires, and plans with an open hand in case He wants to take a new step I had not anticipated.

This was only the beginning of God's program of growth and maturity for me. I realized how important my time in the Word of God was for my dance with Him—it's how He would lead me step-by-step in our adventure. With each move we make together as I respond in faith to His Word, I learn secrets from Him that help me dance better.

One day, as I was perusing the latest books at a Christian bookstore, the thought came very clearly into my mind, *Cath, you need to stop buying books and start writing books.* I stood straight up, realizing my life was about to head in a new direction. I had been thinking about writing for a long time. I was a journal writer from childhood, when I began writing in a Barbie diary. I always loved books and had dreamed of writing a book, but now I wasn't just dreaming—I was compelled to begin writing. God places some desires in our heart that He will fulfill in His own time (Psalm 37:4). Still, I had no idea how to begin writing a book.

The Lord directed me, helping me design a book of quiet times in the Psalms entitled *Pilgrimage of the Heart*. When I finished it, I wondered, *Now, how do I get a publisher?* I sent letters to several publishers and for months received no response. I became confused and frustrated in my endeavor to write a book benefiting others. Then I learned a secret from the Lord that helped me in my next step in the dance—the secret of contentment. Paul said, "I have learned to be content in whatever circumstances I am" (Philippians 4:11). The opposite of contentment is want, what Max Lucado calls a prison filled with those who want something bigger, nicer, faster, and thinner.[2] To be discontent with my situation means I have what I don't want and want what I don't have. I think we all have felt discontent in our lives. Advertisers prey on these feelings, prompting us to buy things we don't need just to satisfy our unfulfilled desires.

Once I learned this secret of contentment, I thought, *How can I live out contentment in not finding a publisher for this book?* All of a sudden, I discovered how to become more resourceful and take a new step in my dance with the Lord. And that's what the Lord Jesus does in our dance—He gives us "outside the box" ideas and takes us on amazing adventures where we catch a glimpse of His glory.

When I realized that not having a publisher for my book was okay with God, it became okay with me too. I decided to publish the book myself by making copies and binding it at an office supply store. I began to experience the fruit of contentment—I was satisfied with dancing with the Lord regardless of my lack or surplus. I was enjoying my dance with the Lord once again—and providing thousands of copies of the book for women all over the world. And in subsequent years, God provided for that book and other books as well.

Are you in a situation that makes you feel discontent? Are you struggling with something you have but don't want or want but don't have?

I surely know that struggle myself. I'm so thankful that the Lord sympathizes with our weakness (Hebrews 4:15-16) and encourages us to draw near to Him for mercy and grace to help us in our time of need. When we lean in to His embrace in our areas of discontent, He helps us in our next step, and the result for a woman whose heart dances with the Lord is contentment. Learning this secret of contentment will help you take the next step of faith in your dance.

After I wrote my first book, I received an invitation from Josh McDowell Ministries to be a guest on Josh's radio show so he could interview me about my book. I was thrilled...we scheduled a date and a time...and then I panicked. *I've never been on the radio before. I can't talk on the radio. What if I make a mistake?* I felt completely inadequate to go on the radio with Josh.

Then I read what God said to Paul in his apparent weakness and inadequacy: "My grace is sufficient for you, for power is perfected in weakness" (2 Corinthians 12:9). Paul concluded, "When I am weak, then I am strong." I read that and thought, *Praise the Lord! I'm weak, and that qualifies me for the power of God!* Since that time, I've noticed that God often leads me step-by-step into situations that are much greater than I can handle. But I've learned the secret of trusting in God's power to help me say, "I can't, but He can."

This lesson of God's strength perfected in our weakness is of huge importance in our dance with the Lord. Have you felt as though you are in a situation that is more than you can handle? I guess we shouldn't be surprised to find ourselves in impossible situations, because the Lord desires to accomplish a work in and through us that only He can do. Hearts that dance with the Lord have learned the secret of weakness, and they lean in to the strong arms of the Lord, relying on His power through the indwelling Holy Spirit. And oh, what results, what amazing dances those in the world will see as they watch from a distance.

If we are to keep in step with the Lord and follow His lead, we must also learn the secret of developing a great trust in Him. I discovered a powerful promise in Psalm 9:10: "Those who know Your name will put their trust in You." One little word was most significant to me: *will*. The Lord showed me that knowing His names—who He is, what He does, and what He says—will lead me to a greater trust in Him. The more I trust Him, the more easily He can lead me in life. You can't trust what you don't know, and what God wants more than anything—in fact, His great desire as we dance with Him—is for us to know Him.

But do we desire to know Him? We should, and if we don't, perhaps John Piper's words will encourage us to step up to a deeper level of desire for God: "If you don't feel strong desires for the manifestation of the glory of God, it is not because you have drunk deeply and are satisfied. It is because you have nibbled so long at the table of the world. Your soul is stuffed with small things, and there is no room for the great."[3] This little secret of knowing and trusting God helped me focus on looking for God every day when I open the Bible. I always look for anything that will help me know my eternal dance Partner better.

Certain steps are common to all dances with the Lord, and you have possibly discovered many of them in your own dance:

- salvation (Ephesians 2:8)
- surrender (Romans 12:1-2)
- spiritual growth and maturity (2 Peter 3:18)
- walking by faith, not sight (2 Corinthians 5:7)
- humility (1 Peter 5:6)
- being filled with the Spirit (Ephesians 5:18)
- praying at all times (Ephesians 6:18)
- living a life of devotion to God and His Word
  (2 Timothy 3:16-17)

These steps are the same for everyone, but God leads us through them in unique ways as we continue to dance with Him, grow, and mature.

On the other hand, some steps in your dance with the Lord will be unusual. That was the case with Mary's display of extravagant love when she seemed to waste a lot of expensive perfume. I remember the day my husband said, "Catherine, I think you should go to seminary."

"Are you kidding?"

"No, I'm serious. You love to study, and I think you should get a degree for all your hard work." I spent the next seven years studying long hours, often wondering why the Lord had led me in such an unusual direction. Now I understand as I see those intense hours reaping fruit in the books I write and the messages I teach.

Sometimes I don't understand the steps the Lord leads me through in our dance. When I stand back and look over the past several years of my life, I just shake my head. How have I kept my head above water? Sometimes in my own dance, I've stumbled under a heavy load of responsibility, working more than one job at a time ever since I was 16 years old. I am ashamed to say that sometimes I've looked at the lives of those around me and wondered, *Why can't I have what they have? Why can't I be like them? Why does my life have to be so hard sometimes?*

Maybe you can relate to my feelings. Of course, we all know that when we look at other people's lives, we never see the whole picture. In fact, sometimes we even admit that those same people occasionally look at us and wish their lives could be like ours. Here's another secret for our dance: I've learned that I need to intentionally keep my eyes fixed on Jesus, following His lead for me and not wanting to be anyone else but the person God has made me to be, for better or for worse.

This prayer by Ann Kiemel helps me accept and even welcome my uniqueness and individuality:

> Jesus, i like what i am because it was Your idea. help me to find adventure in my uniqueness, and not want to be what someone else is. God, if i lose sight of the fun of being me, then Your dreams of what i can be in the world will die. always help me to remember that this is Your way of being creative.[4]

Carol Travilla and Joan Webb share this in their book *The Intentional Woman*: "If I live intentionally, being true to my own personality, serving out of my God-given giftedness and calling, I no longer feel a need to envy anyone else's career, marriage, ministry, talents, or mission."[5] The writer of Hebrews encourages us that when we run our race, we need to fix our eyes on Jesus, the author and perfecter of our faith (Hebrews 12:1-2). Fixing our eyes on Jesus takes intention and purpose every day of our lives.

I love dancing with the Lord, and I am in this adventure of taking steps of faith, one by one, for life—eternal life, that is. There's no looking over my shoulder or turning back. In our goodbye to our old life and hello to our dance with the Lord, we continue to live with some soberness because of the pain in our own lives or in other people's lives. I have become more serious in life, and yet I have an intense joy in my heart. When I find myself in one of those worst-case scenarios that invariably come with the territory, I have to take a deep breath and lean in to the Lord, trusting Him to lead me in the next step even if it includes pain. I'll admit right now that I'm basically a wimp. I hate pain, and I like every circumstance to work out. I love fairy tales, and I want the stories in my life to end "happily ever after." Henri Nouwen offers comforting words of hope for the painful times in our lives:

> We hear an invitation to allow our mourning to become a place of healing, and our sadness a way through pain to dancing...We learn to look fully into our losses, not evade them. By greeting life's pains with something other than denial we may find something unexpected. By inviting God into our difficulties we ground life—even its sad moments—in joy and hope...Ultimately mourning means facing what wounds us in the presence of One who can heal. This is not easy, of course. This dance will not usually involve steps that require no effort. We may need to practice...these steps in the dance of God's healing choreography let us move gracefully amid what would harm us, and find healing as we endure what

could make us despair. We can ultimately find a healing that
lets our wounded spirits dance again, that lets them dance
unafraid of suffering and even death because we learn to live
with lasting hope.[6]

Living with the "now and not yet" of life is another secret of the dance
and rests on the hope of eternal life. Learn to look up, at the horizon, and you will see the light of forever bringing hope in the face of
every seemingly overwhelming frustration. He does indeed turn your
mourning into dancing.

I'm a firm believer in the step-by-step guidance of the Lord in our
dance through the leading of the Holy Spirit, who lives in us. God
cares about a sparrow when it falls to the ground and numbers the
hairs on our head, so surely He is serious about directing the steps
of the godly. His Word promises such meticulous guidance (Psalm
37:23). One of the jobs of the Holy Spirit is to lead us (Romans 8:14).
Why would He give us the Holy Spirit to lead us if He didn't have a
step in mind for us to take?

A woman whose heart dances with the Lord keeps in step with the
Spirit (Galatians 5:25 NIV) and is sensitive to His guidance, moment
by moment. Seeking God's guidance, one step at a time, by asking
Him and waiting for Him to lead, is one of the great secrets we learn
in the dance. I am still learning this secret. I love the way one person
described this secret of God's guidance:

> When I meditated on the word
> GUIDANCE, I kept seeing *dance* at the
> end of the word. I remember
> reading that doing God's will is a lot
> like dancing. When two people
> try to lead, nothing feels right. The
> movement doesn't flow with

the music, and everything is quite
uncomfortable and jerky.
When one person realizes and
lets the other lead, both bodies begin
to flow with the music.
One gives gentle cues, perhaps with a nudge
to the back or by pressing
lightly in one direction or another. It's
as if two become one body,
moving beautifully. The dance takes
surrender, willingness, and
attentiveness from one person and gentle
guidance and skill from the other.
My eyes drew back to the word
GUIDANCE. When I saw "G," I thought of
God, followed by "u" and "i."
"God," "u" and "i" "dance."
God, you and I dance!
This statement is what guidance means to me.
As I lowered my head, I
became willing to trust that I would get
guidance about my life. Once
again, I became willing to let God lead.[7]

Some questions come to mind as we think about following the Lord's guidance in our dance: How can we keep in step with our eternal dance Partner, the Lord Jesus? How can we know what our next step is in our dance with Him? You can know that the Spirit who lives in you always moves in perfect cooperation with God's Word and God's will for you. He knows the next step, and He will lead you.

How can you experience the Holy Spirit's leading in your dance? Very simply, by being filled with the Holy Spirit. When you are filled with the Spirit, you are controlled and empowered by Him rather than dependent solely on your own strength. The filling of the Spirit, a continual experience with the Lord, is essential to a free-flowing, effortless, Jesus-led dance in life. Paul instructs every dancer, "Don't be drunk with wine, because that will ruin your life. Instead, be filled with the Holy Spirit" (Ephesians 5:18 NLT). Henry Morris, the founder of the Institute of Creation Research, says, "Being fully controlled and guided by the Holy Spirit is not just a one-time experience. It *should* be a continual experience—a moment-by-moment control of one's thoughts and actions by God."[8]

How can you be filled (controlled and empowered) by the Holy Spirit? By faith, simply pray, *Lord, fill me with Your Spirit.* I constantly ask the Lord to fill me with His Spirit. When I get ready to teach a Bible study, I pray, *Lord, fill me with Your Spirit.* When I meet with someone for coffee, again I ask, *Lord, fill me with Your Spirit.* When I write a message, an article, or a book, my prayer is, *Lord, fill me with Your Spirit.* And I am confident He is answering my prayer, because His Word assures me He wants to lead me and guide me and fill me with His Spirit, and He promises His favorable response to any requests that are made according to His will (1 John 5:14-15).

How then does the Holy Spirit lead you in the steps of your dance? Often He will use the Bible to show you the way. I like to think of God's Word, filled with precepts and promises, as the training manual for dancing with the Lord. The Bible is filled with virtually thousands of steps, expressed as precepts and promises. The Lord uses His precepts and promises to lead you in your next step in the dance.

His precepts are instructions and principles that help you know how to live your life. One of my favorite passages of Scripture, filled with precepts, is Colossians 3:12-17. This one passage reveals steps for your own dance that you can take with certainty when the need arises, every day of your life. For example, you are encouraged to have a heart of compassion, which means you are to have pity on and show mercy to others. If someone is antagonizing you and trying to stir up an argument, you may be tempted to engage in the strife. But the Lord's step for you is exactly the opposite—show mercy and compassion. When you yield to the Holy Spirit, He will fill you with God's love for the unlovable.

Colossians 3 also encourages you to be kind to others, bearing with them and even profiting them in some way. When someone in your life seems to be competing with you, tearing you down, and diminishing your worth, you can know your next step—the way of Jesus is to offer a gift of kindness.

As Paul continues in this passage, he guides us in the steps of humility, gentleness, patience, forbearance, forgiveness, love, and peace. You can know that when you are filled with the Holy Spirit, you will experience the Spirit's fruit in your life, one step at a time—love, joy, peace, patience, kindness, goodness, faithfulness, gentleness, and self-control (Galatians 5:22-23).

Jesus often leads you in unusual, uncommon actions that pour blessing after blessing on others, eventually drawing them to Himself. Only by living in God's Word and discovering His precepts, one after another, can you truly understand the way of Jesus so you can follow His lead in the dance. When you know the Bible, you know God's heart.

God's promises will keep you in the dance, for they will make the steps easier and lighter, filling you with hope and courage. For example, you may be discouraged because life seems to be passing you by and you can't understand what God is doing in your life. What can encourage you when you encounter such feelings in your dance? Find hope in the promises of Psalm 31:15, "My times are in Your hand" and Psalm 138:8, "The LORD will accomplish what concerns me; your lovingkindness, O LORD, is everlasting; do not forsake the works of your hands." Always carry the promises of God with you and learn as many of them as you can.

You'll never be wasting time when you're discovering God's precepts and promises in His Word. Live in them. Learn them. Memorize them. And then, dear friend, take your next step of faith and dance.

On rare occasions, a dancer steps onto the landscape of history with such grace of movement and glory of faith that everyone stops and watches. Gladys Aylward was just such a dancer. Born into a working class family in London, she aspired to be an actress, but God had something much more important in mind for her. She quit school at the age of 14. She served as a nanny and later as a maid in wealthy households. Although her parents took her to church, she wasn't interested in spiritual things until one night when she attended a religious meeting. She said, "I realized that God had a claim on my life, and I accepted Jesus Christ as my Saviour." Then the steps in her dance began in earnest.

She read an article in a Young Life magazine about China that greatly impressed her. "To realize that millions of Chinese had never heard of Jesus Christ was to me a staggering thought, and I felt we ought to do something about it."[9] God burdened her heart for China in a way that only He can. She applied to the China Inland Mission but was judged unqualified to be a candidate. Thinking the door was closed for her dream, she took another job working in household service. God impressed her heart with the need to know the Bible. She began in Genesis, reading and studying God's Word. When she read Nehemiah, her heart stirred within. It was almost as though she heard a voice: *Gladys Aylward, is Nehemiah's God your God?*

"Yes, of course."

Then do what Nehemiah did, and go.

"But I am not Nehemiah."

No, but I am his God.

She knew she had her marching orders from God. She was going to China. But how would she get there? All she had was a Bible, a copy of *Daily Light*, and a small amount of money. What did she do? She worked for four years and finally saved enough money to go to China. Now the question was, where exactly in China would she go?

She and her mother attended a Methodist meeting and heard of an elderly Scottish widow in China named Mrs. Lawson who had been praying for a young woman to be her assistant. On October 15, 1932, Gladys left her home and her family and set out for China. She didn't see them again for 17 years. Her journey, filled with numerous steps of faith, took her finally to Yangcheng. Her first job in China was to persuade others to stop at Mrs. Lawson's inn so they could hear the gospel of Christ.

At the end of a year, Gladys could understand Chinese and even tell stories in the language. After a year, Mrs. Lawson died, and Gladys was left alone as the sole Westerner in that part of China. She continued leading services at the house and began traveling to surrounding towns to share the gospel.

The steps of her dance then took Gladys in a new direction because Jesus wanted to touch other lives through her. He had His eye on people whom no one else noticed. And that is what He does—He uses us in unexpected places and sometimes in dark places that only He sees.

In the early twentieth century, the Chinese government outlawed the ancient practice of binding the feet of young girls to keep them from growing. No one was hired as foot inspector in the area where Gladys lived, so she was appointed as the official foot inspector and was paid to travel to villages and meet with families there. The Chinese official who appointed her gave her permission to share the gospel because he assumed that those who became Christians would stop the foot binding. Elated, Gladys traveled far and wide, meeting with family after family and sharing the gospel throughout that area of China. She worked to improve prison conditions and gained the name Ai-weh-deh, meaning "virtuous one."

During the war with Japan, her inn became the refuge for about 20 orphans and up to 40 injured soldiers at a time. As the war increased, the number of children she cared for grew to nearly 100. Warned that her life was in danger, she narrowly escaped with the children. She wrote this to her mother during the war years:

> Life is pitiful, death so familiar, suffering and pain so common, yet I would not be anywhere else. Do not wish me out of this or in any way to seek to get me out, for I will not be got out while this trial is on. These are my people. God has

given them to me, and I will live or die with them for him and his glory.[10]

She led her children on a 27-day journey filled with hardship and her own suffering of typhus, pneumonia, malnutrition, and exhaustion. Finally they arrived safely in the province of Sian, some 100 miles away. She began a church and worked in the villages and prisons and among the sick and helpless. Hers was quite a ministry for one turned down by an official mission board as unqualified!

Finally, in 1947, she and other missionaries were forced to leave China by the new Communist regime, and she returned to England for ten years. She then traveled to Taiwan and founded an orphanage, serving God there until her death in 1970. Gladys Aylward touched the lives of more people than we will ever know as she followed the Lord's leading through each step of faith.

And so, as you take one step of faith at a time, your dance will touch the hearts of thousands. The world watches on in wonder. And only heaven will tell the true story of your dance. So, dear friend, step-by-step, follow your Lord and keep on dancing.

Romance

I know what first excited me about the ballet. I fell in love with the romance. Something is so enticing about the music, the filmy flowing costumes, the spectacular leaps and turns, the precision of each step, and the graceful lines of the dancers. I am a great fan of just about any kind of dance, but I especially love classical ballet. The romance of the ballet arises from the winsome story, the lyrical music, the emotional expression coming deep from within the hearts of the dancers, and the integral partnerships of the dancers themselves.

If you watch a performance of one of the great ballets, you will probably see a magnificent love story filled with stunning romance and perhaps a heartrending tragedy. In *Sleeping Beauty*, Princess Aurora was born to a king and queen who had long desired a child. The wicked fairy, Carabosse, visited the birth celebration and announced that Aurora would prick her finger at age 16 and die. The Lilac Fairy came to the rescue and announced that Aurora would not die, but only fall into a deep sleep.

When Aurora turned 16, she received the gift of a beautiful tapestry, sent secretly by the wicked fairy, Carabosse. Woven within the threads was a needle, and Aurora pricked her finger, falling into a deep sleep. One hundred years later, Prince Florimund was hunting with his friends in the forest. The Lilac Fairy met him and gave him a vision of Princess Aurora asleep. He immediately knew she would be his one true love. The Lilac Fairy led Prince Florimund to the hidden castle, where he found Princess Aurora lying asleep. He reached down and kissed her, awaking her from her sleep. The ballet ends as every good fairy tale should. The Prince and Aurora marry, and they live happily ever after.

Sleeping Beauty was the first famous ballet featuring the music of Russian composer Pyotr Ilyich Tchaikovsky. His music lent itself perfectly to this fantasy ballet and has become as popular as the ballet itself. The music, with its engaging rhythms and haunting melodies, is critical to the sense of romance in the dance.

Two of the most famous ballerinas to dance the part of Princess Aurora are Anna Pavlova and Margot Fonteyn. Dancing in *Sleeping Beauty* is traditionally anxiety-provoking, especially in "The Rose Adagio," the scene of Aurora's sixteenth birthday celebration. Fonteyn once asked another dancer, "Maria, do you get nervous about dancing this role?"

"Yes," Maria replied.

Fonteyn replied, "Well, so was I. *Use* your nerves. Turn it all into the role, to give it energy."[1]

A great part of the romance in ballet comes from the heart and passion of the dancer. Anna Pavlova encouraged other dancers to observe people, especially looking into their faces and eyes, in order to discover a new depth for their dance.

> I want you to look at all the faces around you, and you'll see someone who is sad or angry. You must feed yourself through your eyes as well as your ears. If you're going to be an artist, you must do this...You must try to understand why they behave as they do. One day you will dance on the stage, and you must think that if you can make one sad person in the audience happy, even for a moment, you'll begin to be a little bit of an artist.[2]

Ballet is filled with great partnerships—male and female dancing together. Certain ballet moves are impossible without a partner. Clinton Luckett, a teacher for the American Ballet Theatre, described the partnership this way:

> Partnering is mostly about helping the woman maintain her position longer than she could by herself. It's a beautiful demonstration of the male-female dynamic. When you lift a ballerina, you take her physically into space to a place where she can't go alone, and where she wants to go.[3]

In our dance with the Lord, we engage in the greatest love story of all time. We dance to the music of His Word. We experience a sharing of hearts—communion with the One who loves us more than life itself as our heart touches the very heart of God. And finally we enjoy the great partnership with the Prince of Peace, who takes us on the greatest adventure of all, giving us a view we could never have on our own—straight into heaven, where we see the face of God. Every day, moment by moment, the Lord custom-designs our romance with Him, personalizing this dance with joys and experiences He knows will delight our heart.

Romance often includes expressions custom-designed for specific occasions. I recently saw this romance of life communicated in a birth announcement from some dear friends, a fellow author and his family, for their new baby girl, Audrey. I wish you could see the colorful picture and meticulous design. Clearly, the parents put a lot of care into this announcement, showing just how proud they are of their new gift from the Lord.

When God's Son made His entrance on the human scene of earth, God fashioned magnificent birth announcements that were initially private but then made public in His Word. They continue to impact our lives to this day. God didn't send out paper announcements. Instead, He wrote His announcement in the sky with a star, communicating the wonder of the birth of His Son to the Magi—astrologers and phi-losophers who visited Jesus in Bethlehem to worship Him. And God didn't announce the birth of His Son in church. Instead, He sent an angel and a heavenly choir to shepherds to praise and glorify God, saying "Glory to God in the highest, and on earth peace to men on whom his favor rests" (Luke 2:13-14 NIV).

One elderly woman received a birth announcement from the Lord that was custom-designed just for her, and she was called by God to a special place of service as a result. Imagine Anna's excitement decades earlier when she was first married and had her whole life ahead of her. Dreams filled her mind of perhaps children, family, and a loving and warm home. But everything she imagined for her future crumbled into dust when, after only seven years, her husband died. Now she was a widow, something she would never have imagined for herself. This was her great sadness.

As in all the greatest sadness, we can be bitter or better, disappointed or devoted, resentful or rejoicing, pitiful or prayerful. Anna was a special girl with a heart for God and devotion to her Lord. She danced with Him. Knowing the wonder of silence in communion with God, she chose the dance. Though deeply hurt, she loved God deeper still. She became a woman of worship—skilled in fasting, prayer, and devotion to God. In her dance with the Lord, she discovered a special connec-tion to the heart of God—a sharing of His heart that only those called to be prophets can know. She carried with her the title of prophetess and was known for receiving special revelations from God.

News came one day that Herod was going to build a temple for the Jews, allowing them to worship God. After ten years of the tireless labor of more than 1000 priests trained as masons to build the struc-ture, the main building loomed large on the landscape of Jerusalem. When Anna looked at the white porticoes, she must have sensed God drawing her in to His house to serve Him as His woman for such a time as this. Daily she walked through four rows of columns and past Solomon's porch. She watched the scribes debating in their schools among the colonnades, and she wondered that at one time this area had been just dust and rubble.

Years passed, and Anna continued walking in God's house, magnificent and holy—at least that's how it felt to her. She regarded the temple as a house of prayer (Isaiah 56:7). She came to love the Court of Women, for it was her home, day and night. She never left the temple— she lived a life of devotion there, consistently fasting and praying.

Clearly she lived during a time when her people were in trouble. Oppressed by the Romans, they had but one hope—the promised Messiah, who would come from God and save His people. He was known as the consolation of Israel and would bring salvation and redemption.

As a prophetess, Anna knew of the promised Messiah. He was often the subject of her prayers and fasting. Perhaps she prayed something like this: *Lord, when will You redeem us? Send the Promised One, the Christ. He is our great hope.* With a burdened heart, she fasted, hungering only for God Himself to meet her in the deepest places of her soul. She talked often with her Lord, pouring out her soul to Him year after year.

From heaven, the eyes of the Lord searched to and fro, looking deep into the hearts of His people. And of all the people whose hearts He saw, He chose two for special demonstrations of His love. One was Simeon, a man in Jerusalem, who was righteous and devout and was looking for the consolation of Israel. And the other was Anna, the blessed widow who loved God and was devoted to Him. As a result, they both experienced the blessed romance of the dance.

Who can know what the day was like—perhaps the sun was shining or a bit of rain had fallen. But this was the day that Mary and Joseph brought their beloved newborn Son, Jesus, to the temple to present Him to God, an act prescribed by law. They walked through the columns and porticoes of the temple and saw an older man approaching them. He walked up to them and held out his hands. Mary and Joseph were becoming used to such unusual attention to their child.

Somehow sensing this was a special moment from God, they handed their newborn Son to this man. Simeon took Him into his arms, blessed God, and prayed.

> Now Lord, You are releasing Your bond-servant to depart in peace, according to Your word; for my eyes have seen Your salvation, which You have prepared for all peoples, a light of revelation to the Gentiles, and the glory of Your people Israel (Luke 2:29-32).

Mary and Joseph had seen adoration and worship of their Son, but now they were amazed at what Simeon said about Him. Simeon, in the Spirit, blessed both Mary and Joseph.

And then came the moment when God was to give His precious servant Anna, who could have been named "faithful one" for her faithfulness to God, a special gift she would never forget. For at the very moment Simeon was blessing Mary and Joseph, Anna walked up and joined them. She took one look at this baby and knew His identity. And oh, how she was filled with thankfulness to her Lord. He had answered her deepest prayers and showed her the fulfillment of her heart's desire. She knew He didn't have to do it, but she also knew He had designed this for her, allowing her to see the Messiah.

And with that glimpse, she became God's messenger. What she had seen moved her to a new area of service. She became the voice of proclamation, telling all who were looking for the Messiah that He had come and that she had seen Him with her own eyes. Only God could have orchestrated the meeting of Anna and Christ the Messiah, the Promised One. Anna knew this, and she thanked God over and over again.

That's what God does. He sees your heart and custom-designs expressions of love from His heart to yours. That's the romance of the dance.

— ❋ —

I'm a romantic. I admit it. I love to watch romantic movies (even if guys *do* call them chick flicks). Yes, I love them. Tell me about a romantic love story, and I'm the first one in line to watch it. I've thrilled to the love stories of Rhett and Scarlett in *Gone With the Wind*, Rafe and Evelyn in *Pearl Harbor*, the Captain and Maria in *The Sound of Music*, and Rick and Ilsa in *Casablanca*, just to name a few. I have watched all of these movies more than once and could be considered a movie buff. I especially like the movies with happy endings.

When I married, I discovered my husband also is a romantic. On one of my birthdays early in our marriage, I awoke to find an elegantly wrapped present on our bed. At just that moment, my entertaining husband came in with a birthday cake (white with white icing, just the way I like it), singing, "Happy birthday to you, happy birthday to you, happy birthday dear Catherine, the one I love with all my heart, happy birthday to you." I laughed and clapped my hands with glee. I was loving this celebration presented by my loving husband.

"Open your present," he said. I tore the ribbon from the white box, pulled back the tissue paper, and caught my breath. It was an emerald green silk robe. Of course, I immediately put it on, tying the green silk sash tightly around my waist. I ran to the mirror, admiring my newfound elegance.

"Open the card, Cath!" my husband eagerly urged. I ripped open the envelope and pulled out a small glossy card. Opening it, this is what I read: "You are invited to attend dinner tonight with David Martin at…" Below the dots was a yellow Post-it note covering the location. The words written on top of it were, "Pull here to discover the location of dinner."

I looked at my smiling husband. "What have you done now?" Pulling off the yellow paper, I read, "The Grille at the Hotel St. Francis, San Francisco, California."

And just at that very moment, my husband whipped out an airline folder. "And here are the tickets! Now pack your bags. We leave in three hours!"

"Whoo-hoo!" I shouted. Excitedly I jumped up and hugged and kissed him. "Honey, this is the best gift in the whole wide world. I can't wait. Thank you for being my husband." I feel so blessed that the Lord brought us together.

Paul compares the love between a man and a woman in marriage to the love relationship Christ has with those of us who dance with Him. In fact, believers are called the church and the bride of Christ in the Bible (Ephesians 5:25). We see that the Lord nourishes and cherishes us, demonstrating how precious we are to Him in our dance. Our relationship with Him is truly a love story of epic proportions. He died in our place, sacrificing His life so we might live with Him forever. You can know that you mean everything to Him. He truly romances us, wooing us to Himself each day.

In fact, the Bible is God's love letter, and in it, you discover His overtures again and again: "Be still, and know that I am God" (Psalm 46:10 NIV). "You will seek Me and find Me when you search for Me with all your heart. I will be found by you" (Jeremiah 29:13-14). "Come to Me, all who are weary and heavy-laden, and I will give you rest" (Matthew 11:28). Henri Nouwen writes his response to the Lord's invitation to come to Him:

> Lord…Your heart is so full of the desire to love me, so aflame with a fire to warm me. You so much want to give me a home, a sense of belonging, a place to dwell, a shelter where I feel protected and a refuge in which I feel safe. You stand at so many squares and corners of my life and say with so much tenderness, "Come and see, come and stay with me. When you are thirsty, come to me…you who put your trust in me, come and drink. Come, you who are tired, exhausted, depressed, discouraged and dispirited. Come, you who feel pain in your body, fatigue in your anxious mind and doubt and anguish in the depth of your heart. Come and know that I have come to give you a new heart and a new spirit"…
>
> I am looking at you, Lord. You have said so many loving words.

Your heart has spoken so clearly...O Lord, how can I ever go anywhere else but to you to find the love I so desire!...O dear Jesus, your heart is only love. I see you; I hear you; I touch you. With all my being, I know that you love me.[4]

In Nouwen's words, you see how a heart that dances can respond to the wooing of the Lord in our lives. The Lord is always saying, in every circumstance, *Will you dance with Me?* Hear His invitation and respond, *Yes, Lord, I will dance with You.* Every day when you open your Bible, pray, *Lord, speak with me this morning. I want to dance with You.* Understand that life is all about your dance with the Lord. When you begin to see your life this way, you will experience a new sense of the romance between you and your Lord.

Let me ask you, is there something special going on between you and the Lord? I want to encourage you to enlarge your vision and to begin cultivating your romance with the Lord. Dance, dear friend, dance. David was determined in his dance with the Lord. He said, "I will celebrate before the LORD" (2 Samuel 6:21). We must freely and wholeheartedly celebrate Him even if no one else in our life does.

I have two friends, a husband and wife from Vietnam, who run a beauty salon in our neighborhood. I love to watch them work together as they sit side-by-side at their manicure stations. While the husband is at work, he will speak softly to his wife. She responds softly. I cannot hear or understand what they are saying, but I love to watch them enjoy an intimate, constant, back-and-forth conversation. One day I watched them walk across the parking lot together. She was holding his arm as they walked and talked with each other.

We can engage in this same kind of intimate, ongoing conversation with our Lord. Prayer is meant to be a constant communion as we "pray continually" (1 Thessalonians 5:17 NIV). Softly whispering to our Lord as we walk and talk with Him, we enjoy the privilege and the romance of dancing with Him.

David, our great example in the dance, shows us how tenacious we must be to preserve and enjoy our romance with the Lord. When his wife saw him dancing with all his might before the Lord, she "despised him in her heart" (2 Samuel 6:16). She made fun of him, saying, "How the king of Israel distinguished himself today!" David responded, "I will celebrate before the LORD" (2 Samuel 6:20-21). Our romance with the Lord includes a resolve to celebrate Him in our dance.

I love celebrating my Lord as we dance together. I do crazy things because I am crazy in love with Him. Sometimes I'll have breakfast with Him at one of my favorite coffeehouses. I get my coffee and my breakfast sandwich. Then I find my favorite table—quiet and in a corner—and sit with open Bible and my *Quiet Time Notebook*. I write in my journal something like this: "Lord, I love being here with You. What do You have to say to me today? I am ready to dance."

I've also been known to buy a bouquet of flowers for my Lord. I put them on my desk and write the card out to Him, celebrating Him through the whole day. When I go away to write, I celebrate special lunches and dinners with Him. I like to light a candle in my quiet time sometimes just to remind me that He is the light of the world and the light in my life, bringing His light into every dark experience I may encounter.

I have a plaque that displays three words: "Believe, Dream, Imagine." These words remind me to believe God, dream big, and imagine what He can do in my romance with Him. Whenever I become discouraged or disheartened, these words keep me focused on my dance with the Lord. I remember to believe Him instead of faltering in my faith. I remember to dream big, as Henrietta Mears used to say, because anything less than a great dream is just too small for our great God. And finally, in my romance with the Lord, I like to follow the example of David by imagining what God can do and eagerly watching to see Him at work (Psalm 5:3). Believing God, cultivating great dreams, and imagining the fulfillment of God's promises help fan the flame of love in our hearts for our eternal dance Partner.

⸺ ✳ ⸺

I believe the Lord delights in giving us special gifts, tailor-made for us. We know that "every good thing given and every perfect gift is from above, coming down from the Father of lights, with whom there is no variation or shifting shadow" (James 1:17). I recently read a note from a woman who was a Bible study leader and who had just learned about *El Elyon*, one of the names of God. Here's what she wrote:

> The neatest thing God did for me was just a couple of weeks ago when my own father was visiting. I had been pondering on the name *El Elyon* for a couple of days. It meant so much to me to remember that God is indeed sovereign over every single thing in my life. As one who has dealt with fear all my life, this truth brought a calming effect to my soul. Well, my dad and I were at a local jewelry store that specializes in Christian items and I noticed a simple silver key chain that had engraved on it "El Elyon." It was $20 and I had to have it! I asked the woman for it and my father, who was purchasing a birthday present for my oldest daughter, said "Put that in with my stuff." It was a double blessing—a gift from both my heavenly Father and my earthly one. Love that!

I love this story because it is so demonstrative of the romantic heart of our Lord. Only God knew that this woman had just learned His name *El Elyon* and then gave her a key chain with that name on it. I've never even heard of a key chain with any name of God engraved on it, let alone *El Elyon*, the very name of God this woman had just studied. And yet the Lord moved heaven and earth to give this precious woman just such a gift. That gift from God blesses my heart.

The Lord permeates our lives, and at unexpected turns, He showers us with unique expressions of love. Again and again I have seen Him demonstrate such amazing acts of love in my own life. I see His hand at work, constantly adding romance to our relationship.

One day I traveled to Dallas to speak at a women's conference and attended a luncheon hosted by the church leaders. I remember walking up to the door of the house, anticipating the new women I would meet. Imagine my surprise as I walked into the room and was surrounded by dozens of women who felt close to me because they had used my studies in their ministry for several years. Instantly, we were friends, with a deep bond of love. I whispered softly to the Lord, *This is You, isn't it, Lord! You have given me a special demonstration of Your love. You wanted me to know these blessed women with such incredible hearts for the Lord. Oh, how You are at work in places unknown to me. Thank You, Lord.*

On another day I was shopping in a department store, trying to find something stylish and elegant for a speaking engagement but striking out. I couldn't find anything that was right and within my budget. I was ready to give up and go home. I turned the corner in the dressing room and noticed a very classy-looking woman with blonde hair, black pants, a white shirt, and a khaki vest standing at the entrance. She struck up a conversation with me, asking about my ministry. Then she said words that I could hardly believe: "Catherine, this is your special day. I put together designer fashion shows for major department stores. Tell you what I'm going to do. I am going to be your personal stylist, no charge. I will put together all your outfits for you." Again I said, *This is You, Lord, isn't it! Thank You, Lord.* Only Jesus cares about such details, and He put together this special demonstration of love just for me.

I'll never forget the time I opened my Bible in my quiet time and read the first four words of Genesis 8:1: "But God remembered Noah." God spoke volumes to me that day in those seemingly simple words. He used them to remind me that our sorrows do pass, and He lavishes His love and care on us. He filled my heart with a new hope after a deep time of despair in my own pilgrimage with Him. He reminded me that a new day always follows a dark night. And in that overture through His Word, I experienced the romance in our dance. I whispered to my Lord, barely able to hold back tears, *This is You, isn't it!*

Thank You, Lord, for encouraging me today. Only You could have known the deep pain I have felt. And only You could have spoken from these words, filling my heart with a new hope.

And what about the day I received a letter from a young man who was in prison and feeling hopeless? He found *Walking with the God Who Cares,* my book on hope and the promises of God, in the prison library and was encouraged by it. Only the Lord knew how such an event in this young man's life would bless my heart. Again I said, *Lord, You did this, didn't You. Thank You, Lord.*"

Things happen that some people would call good luck or serendipity. Most would say, "What a coincidence." To those people I reply, "It's the Lord. It's His romance in the dance." John, the beloved disciple, understood the romance. When he and the disciples caught an uncommon number of fish after not catching any all night, John said, "It is the Lord" (John 21:7). A woman whose heart dances with the Lord looks for the romance and recognizes His loving overtures, saying, "It is the Lord."

I love one of the scenes near the end of the movie *The Chronicles of Narnia: The Lion, the Witch and the Wardrobe.* Lucy wonders where Aslan is going away to, and Mr. Tumnus explains by simply saying, "He's not a tame lion."

Lucy responds, "No...but he is good."

That description helps me remember the truth about my Lord in our romance—He is the Lion of the tribe of Judah (Revelation 5:5), and He will lead in our dance as He so desires. His wildness is part of the romance, for you never know what new overture He will make toward you. And you can count on His goodness and His love.

Keep your eyes open, my friend. Just when you least expect it, you will see the Lord giving you a present, something just for you. When you recognize His act of love, romancing you in the dance, say, *Thank You, Lord,* and celebrate Him.

10

Story

I stood nervously behind two other dancers, hidden by the props on the left of the stage, all of us waiting for our cue. I was excited but scared. I was only 12, and though I had taken ballet lessons for six years, I hadn't danced on pointe in a live production. I had dreamed of this moment for many years. We were at Phoenix Little Theater, and the curtain was about to rise. Suddenly I thought, *I can't believe I'm finally going to dance on toe shoes here at this theater!*

I heard the music swell and knew we were about to step onstage in front of the audience. The familiar strains of the music seemed to propel us into action. Now my mind was on one thing only—how I would perform the choreographed steps and movements in perfect harmony with the music. I had practiced so many times that I knew the dance by heart. And the hours of practice resulted in a perfect performance—no mistakes!

At the end of the play, the applause brought all of us out onto the stage. I curtsied the way our dance teacher had taught us and looked out into the audience. They were smiling, obviously pleased with the play and our performance. As I ran off stage, I thought, *What a joy to perform for so many people. It's just like a fairy tale.*

In ballet, every dance tells a story of tragedy and triumph. And though sadness is sometimes a part of the story, the grace and movement of the dancers bring a certain satisfaction to the audience. In ballets like *Giselle* and *Swan Lake*, the heroes and heroines die in the end. But the music and dance tell a story that touches the lives of those watching well beyond the fall of the curtain. So too, when you dance with God, He brings a message through the joys and sorrows of the story of your life. Your life proclaims to the world God's existence and His great glory and power.

From before the foundation of the world, God dreamed of His dance with a very special young woman. He referred to His dance with her many years before the determined day of her birth. Following the sin of Adam and Eve, God alluded to the story He would tell in her life by speaking of the child she would bear (Genesis 3:15). He disclosed a little more of her life story in Isaiah 7:14: "Behold, a virgin will be with child and bear a son, and she will call His name Immanuel." But many years would pass before those words were fulfilled.

Finally, the day arrived for God to reveal the special story that this young woman would tell through her dance with Him (Luke 1:26-38). In the town of Nazareth in Galilee, Mary, who was probably only about 16 years of age, had just embarked on the most exciting time of her life. She was betrothed to Joseph, who was probably about 18. She knew this betrothal was serious business, more binding than our present-day engagements. Joseph had declared his commitment to her, and now, their pledge to each other could be terminated only by a divorce.

Mary loved God and wanted to honor Him in everything, including her marriage to Joseph. She, like most 16-year-old girls, probably had filled her heart with hopes for a home and family.

But now she was going to receive an invitation to dance on a new stage in a way no other girl or woman had ever danced before. She could never maneuver the steps in this dance alone, but God Himself would lead her through the power of the Holy Spirit. And so, on a day that may have begun very much like any other day for Mary, the angel Gabriel suddenly appeared to her.

"Greetings, favored one! The Lord is with you."

She had never heard anyone speak like that. What could such words mean for someone like her? In fact, who would ever say such things? She could not even begin to understand this greeting and began shaking with fear.

The angel said to her, "Don't be afraid Mary; for you have found favor with God. And behold, you will conceive in your womb and bear a son, and you shall name Him Jesus."

The angel explained the identity of her child with descriptions that overwhelmed her. But as the reality of what he was saying began to sink in, one big question came into her mind. "How can this be, since I am a virgin?" Good question from a 16-year-old girl betrothed and ready to marry. She did not yet realize the ramifications of this message from God. Now God was going to make His new overture in His dance with Mary.

"The Holy Spirit will come upon you, and the power of the Most High will overshadow you; and for that reason the holy Child shall be called the Son of God." Then, sharing additional miraculous news, he said, "And behold, even your relative Elizabeth has also conceived a son in her old age."

This angel, whose very presence was incredible enough, was revealing one unbelievable piece of information after another. How could Mary fathom all she was seeing and hearing? She would become pregnant as a virgin through the miraculous power of the Holy Spirit... that must have been more than her mind could comprehend. Then came the promise of all promises, something she could hold on to when she was tempted to doubt: "For nothing will be impossible with God."

How did Mary respond? Did she pack her bags and run away, knowing a pregnancy without a marriage would cause a terrible scandal? Did she fall into despair, realizing her betrothal to Joseph was in jeopardy? Did she just sit down and give up, knowing her plans for her future had just gone up in a puff of smoke?

Mary was a woman with a heart that dances. She leaned in, surrendered, and said, with her words and actions, *Yes, Lord, I will dance with You.* She responded, "Behold, the bondslave of the Lord; may it be done to me according to your word." What risky and gutsy words for such a young girl! But Mary was a dancer. She believed God—as do all dancers when God calls them to a new stage in the dance. Her stage was that of the impossible and unbelievable. Trusting the Lord, she danced with Him.

Elizabeth, Mary's elder cousin, rejoiced when she saw Mary dancing with the Lord: "Blessed is she who believed that there would be a fulfillment of what had been spoken to her by the Lord" (verse 45). Here we see God giving Mary a message of faith and trust in a seemingly impossible situation.

Think about Mary's dance. What a story the Lord told through her life! She trusted God to lead her through every step in her dance with Him—raising Jesus, faithfully loving her husband, and watching her Son, Jesus, suffer an unjust crucifixion. Her dance was filled with great joys and incredibly deep sorrows, some that broke her heart in ways no other woman would ever know. But she said yes to the dance. And the story of her life has encouraged millions of men and women to believe God's promises, treasure His words, trust Him when they don't understand why, and rely on Him for comfort in their deepest sorrows. That's the power of the story of your dance with the Lord—when you lean in and say yes, your life speaks to others in ways you will see and understand only when you step from time into eternity.

Everyone loves a good story, and I am no exception. As a little girl, I curled up next to my mother while she read to me from the book *Ellen Tebbits* by Beverly Cleary. One adventure in particular is so memorable to me—the story of Ellen riding a horse for the first time. My mother and I read that passage out loud together. I'll never forget my mother reading the section about the horse refusing to cross the stream. When the horse turned around and looked back at Ellen as though she were crazy, Mother and I laughed until tears rolled down our cheeks. If I hadn't known it before, I learned right then and there how much I loved the stories written in books.

The first time I read The Chronicles of Narnia, I read all seven books in one weekend. These stories by C.S. Lewis, a brilliant thinker as well as writer, were so exciting that I couldn't wait to find out what happened next. Masterfully written page-turners always make you want to find out how the story will unfold.

As good as the stories in books can be, one story is even better— the story that the Lord tells through your dance with Him. He is the Master storyteller. No one can write a message in a life the way He can. In fact, He is making your life a page-turner even now. And He has dreamed of your story from before the foundation of the world. In 2 Corinthians 3:3, the apostle Paul says his readers are "a letter of Christ...written not with ink but with the Spirit of the living God, not on tablets of stone but on tablets of human hearts." This letter is "known and read by all men" (verse 2).

I love this new perspective—Jesus is writing a story in and through our lives as we dance together with Him. And what is the message He proclaims when we dance? To use another metaphor, He spreads the sweet-smelling aroma of the knowledge of Himself in every place (2 Corinthians 2:14). F.B. Meyer says, "Every Christian should be a clearly written and legible tract, circulating for the glory of God. Men will not read the evidences for Christianity contained in learned treatises, but they are keen to read us." People watch our lives, and they notice when we're living in God's power and strength. They see Jesus in us. And when they see Him, they are drawn to Him and want to know Him.

Maybe you're thinking, *How can that be? My life is just average. It's nothing special. As a matter of fact, I'm in such a difficult place, I can barely keep my head above water.* Friend, be patient in the midst of your trial when you dance with Him through impossibly difficult places. Watch to see how He leads you. He is sharing His message in a unique way through the story of your life. No one is average when she dances with the Prince of Peace, King of kings, and Lord of lords.

How can our dance with the Lord become an adventurous page-turner? Paul's words in 2 Corinthians 2:14-15 (NLT) help us understand how He delivers a powerful message through our lives. "Thank God! He has made us his captives and continues to lead us along in Christ's triumphal procession. Now he uses us to spread the knowledge of Christ everywhere, like a sweet perfume. Our lives are a Christ-like fragrance rising up to God."

Captives of Christ

First, we see that the Lord makes us His captives. The Greek word here means "to lead in triumph" and gives us the image of a general who parades his captives through his own city as he celebrates a great victory. As Jesus' captives, we die to ourselves and are now alive to Him, belonging ever and only to Him. This means that God is the Author of the story of your life, not you. You are His. Your story will develop naturally as you release control and allow Him to make a page-turner of your life. You may want to write one kind of story, and He may have something completely different in mind. No wonder Paul said, "I die daily" (1 Corinthians 15:31). We must die to self in order to live to Christ—this is an essential in living the "crucified life." Paul says, "I have been crucified with Christ; and it is no longer I who live, but Christ lives in me; and the life which I now live in the flesh I live by faith in the Son of God, who loved me and gave Himself up for me" (Galatians 2:20).

A Surprising Story

Your life story is filled with chapters, and each one is designed by the Lord. Sometimes those chapters will include surprises. When we remember that God is the Author and that He is in control of the story of our lives, we are more likely to release control to Him and let Him write the message He wants to convey. David's words in Psalm 138:8 (NLT) help us trust God as He writes the story of our lives and choreographs it in our dance with Him: "The LORD will work out His plans for my life—for your faithful love, O LORD, endures forever."

Victors in Christ

God makes our lives page-turners by leading us in Christ's victory parade. Regardless of what we face, we can know victory because of Christ. Paul says, "Thanks be to God, who gives us the victory through our Lord Jesus Christ" (1 Corinthians 15:57). Even when we pass from this life to the next, we experience victory, for then we are face-to-face with our Lord forever in eternity. As the Lord develops the story of your life from one chapter to the next, don't be surprised if the plot includes some baffling twists and turns. Look at Paul's life—his story often included persecution and suffering. And though he suffered, God delivered him in astounding and miraculous ways. What a page-turner his life was! And he must have endured his trials with joy, because when he shared the story of his life, "the disciples were continually filled with joy and with the Holy Spirit" (Acts 13:52).

Always remember that victory is written all over the pages of your life because Jesus, your dance Partner, is Victor. I don't know how He will write the victory in the midst of your circumstance, whatever it may be. Just remember the Lord's great power, His strength, and His amazing creative ability in and through you. Just when you think it's over, it's not over, because God is at work. He has a plan and a purpose for you (see Ephesians 2:10).

A Story for Others to Read

Your life becomes a page-turner of an adventure because God makes Christ known to others through you. The Lord will use your story to bring others to Himself. Oh, how exciting these divine appointments are in life! I was at a truck stop one day at about six in the morning and met a girl in jeans and a black leather jacket with the most interesting belt. The buckle was a silver heart. "I love your belt," I said. "I love the heart."

"I like the heart too," she replied.

"You know what? Life is all about the heart. In fact, God doesn't look at the outward appearance, He looks at hearts. Everywhere. All over the world. He sees hearts."

"I know. And He'll find us, won't He."

"Yes," I answered. "As a matter of fact, Jesus found a woman at a well, and He saw the life she had been living and the hunger in her heart. And He gave her new life."

"Someone told me that when you meet Jesus, He makes a lady out of you."

Tears came to my eyes when she said that. "You know what? That's exactly what He does. He changes us. Makes us holy, righteous, and good." I smiled at her and said, "God bless you. I'll never forget what you said today."

"I won't either," she replied.

Oh, what page-turners our lives become when we realize that the Lord is touching other lives through us. Our lives are page-turners because Jesus lives in us. People see His love, His joy, His peace, His patience, and His kindness in our lives. His presence in you makes your life a unique story.

Living in the Audience of God

And finally, our lives become page-turners as we live in the audience of God. Paul was confident that "God is watching us" (2 Corinthians 2:17 NLT). God is with us, and He never leaves us or forsakes us. He is constantly busy writing His story on our hearts.

—❖—

What will help you to keep in step with the leading and guiding of the Holy Spirit as He writes the story of your life? How can your life become a page-turner that God uses to change other lives?

- *Believe* in God's plan and purpose for your life. You have hope and a future.

- *Pray* for those you know and those you don't know who don't know Jesus.

- *Build* your life on the authority of God and His Word. Always ask, what does God say? Then spend daily quiet time in the Bible.

- *Learn* to share the gospel with others.

- *Look* for opportunities to share your faith.

- *Listen* to the cries of people's hearts.

- *Share* the love of God with everyone you meet.

- *Watch* what God will do!

What can you know about the story God is telling in and through you? Your story is unique because you are one of a kind. The Lord has ordained your days and has a plan for your life. Paul explains in Ephesians 2:10 (NLT) that you are "God's masterpiece." God created you anew in Christ Jesus so that you can accomplish all that He planned for you long ago. God's message through you will speak of the knowledge of Jesus everywhere you go and in everything you do.

Understanding that God is telling a story through your dance also helps you make sense of the people and circumstances in your life. Throughout our lives, God causes certain people to cross our paths. For me, one of these unique friendships was with Leann Pruitt McGee, a staff member with Campus Crusade who discipled me at Arizona State University. Where would I be today if Leann had not taught me how to share my faith, study the Bible, and have a quiet time? These are the basic steps in my dance with the Lord. They help me enact stories of devotion to God and commitment to Christ.

Who would I be today had I not experienced countless precious times together with my mother, one of my best friends? My story would be so different without the long conversations I enjoy with my brother, Robert—another of my best friends. And what about the many meetings at coffee shops and restaurants with special heart-friends, my dear sisters in the Lord who love to share the Word of God with me? As your heart dances with the Lord, He will weave friends, conversations, and experiences into your life story.

God has uniquely designed you as a woman of purpose and design. Your days are included in His plan, from your birth until you are face-to-face with Him. David says in Psalm 139:16 (NLT), "Every day of my life was recorded in your book." Do you see the beauty of David's affirmation of truth? God thought about your days before they even occurred. No wonder David, the great dancer, concluded that his times were in God's hand (Psalm 31:15) and that the Lord would accomplish what concerned him (Psalm 138:8).

I believe in the sovereign hand of God at work in our lives. I like to imagine the Lord reaching out His hand to us and whisking us onto the dance floor, leading us in a dance of His own design. The dance becomes an adventure. Sometimes we can understand where He is leading us and what He is designing for us, and at other times His moves are not so apparent. Sometimes the dance is slow and methodic. And sometimes the moves are so rapid we can barely keep in step with Him. But always, throughout it all, He is inviting us to dance.

I recently read this description of the common struggle of finding our place in life:

> We all have different roles to play, but most of us don't even know where to start. Some of us feel like foreigners in a strange land, knowing that we were made for greatness. Others have given up the search and camped out in a world in which their

passions and talents do not fit, conforming to what they see around them, silently screaming inside. Most of us, I think, fall somewhere in between, unsure of what is to come and discontent with what has been, desperately restless in our spirits for true adventure, beauty, and intimacy.[1]

What role is God calling you to embrace as He leads you on your dance with Him? My own passion is for personal spiritual revival in the lives of those in the church of Jesus Christ. I want to see others get excited about their dance with the Lord, lean in, open His Word, and draw near through quiet time with Him. When I step from time into eternity, I'd love for my tombstone to read, "She touched the hem of His garment, and she danced with Him."

I wonder what story the Lord is telling through your life. What are the movements of your dance? How does your own family fit in—your parents, siblings, spouse, children? Who are the friends God has brought into your life? What unusual twists and turns has He choreographed in your dance with Him? When you stop to think about the answers to these questions, you will understand more about God's purpose in and through your life. You may even want to devote some pages in your journal or notebook just to think through the joys, the victories, and the challenges you have experienced.

The times of suffering often make no sense at all, and yet we still dance, and God continues to write His story on the pages of our lives. George Watson says, "There are innumerable degrees of suffering among God's chosen ones, yet in each case it is unique and personal. The ingredients of suffering are of infinite variety in kind and mixture, but the end to be accomplished is the same." He continues by saying that we sometimes wash the cross we carry in life "thousands of times with our tears" and are, at last, "conquered and mellowed and sweetened into utter tenderness of spirit."[2]

I witnessed firsthand the sweet, precious spirit of one who was experiencing the pain of watching her child suffer. I walked by her in Bible study one day and asked in passing, "How are you? I haven't seen you for a while."

"I'm okay," she replied.

And then I stopped and looked into her eyes. She wasn't okay. "What's wrong?"

Tears spilled onto her face, and she told me about her daughter's illness. We cried and prayed together. In the crucible of her fiery ordeal, she cried, "It just doesn't seem to make sense." But then she continued, "I know God holds us all in His hand and that He will work out His plan. I think I understand Romans 8:28 in a whole new way, for I am growing closer to God through all of this."

Everything in your life means something. God is weaving a story, His story, in and through you. Your purpose in the dance with Him is to know Him and love Him and glorify Him. You may not always realize or understand all that the Lord is doing in your life. In fact, you will probably wonder at times how He can possibly use you in the face of certain failures or impossible situations.

When I experience times like that, I find it helpful to focus again on my purpose and mission in life. In fact, I even take time again to write out the things I'm most passionate about and that spur me on in my dance with the Lord. In this book I've shared vignettes from my own dance with the Lord so I could help you see the story God tells in a life, even one as simple as my own.

I love to think about our lives as tapestries. We see the underside with all the knots and different colors of threads, even the darkest of threads. But God sees the upper side and the beautiful picture He is weaving in our lives. He has the uncanny and miraculous ability to take every thread and weave it into a beautiful picture that tells a unique story of His glory and grace. In fact, He promises to weave things together for all who love Him and are called according to His purpose—for women with hearts that dance: "And we know that God causes all things to work together for the good to those who love Him and are called according to His purpose" (Romans 8:28). Keep your eyes open, dear friend, for the next step in your dance, and know that everything is working together for God's purpose so that He can tell His great story—the story of His existence, His grace, and His glory—in and through your life.

Lord, I Can't Wait to See Your Face

11

Surprise

A young woman walked up to me at our Quiet Time Ministries resource table, engaging me with her warm smile. "Catherine, could I talk with you for a moment?"

I looked into eyes bright with joy and the love of Jesus. "Sure, let's talk over here," I said, gesturing to the side of the table. "What's your name?"

"Kathleen Rousar. I lead a group of women through one of your studies, *A Heart That Dances.* And I'd like to ask permission from you to send you something."

"Well, of course. No problem. I'd love to hear from you. Here's my address."

A few weeks later, I excitedly opened a package from Kathleen and pulled out a small book of pages tied with a satin ribbon. *What's this?* I wondered, enjoying this mysterious present. I ceremoniously untied the ribbon, turned a page, and gasped. An elegant painting of a ballerina adorned the first page. This was no average piece of artwork. The style of painting evoked deep emotion in me. I began slowly turning the pages, one by one, and each page revealed a different painting of ballet dancers in different positions with different expressions. Grace and beauty washed through each painting. Tears welled up in my eyes and began rolling down my face. *These are women with hearts that dance!* The Lord surprised me in such a personalized, loving way through Kathleen's depictions of what it means to dance with Him.

And that is what our Lord does when we dance with Him—He surprises us with personalized expressions of His love for us. David, our example of a dancing heart, knew this. David never told God about his needs and then stopped praying. He told God his concerns, and then, according to Psalm 5:3, he eagerly watched. This means he was waiting and watching closely to see what God would do. He knew God loved to surprise him, and he couldn't wait to see each new surprise. A woman with a heart that dances knows her God is a God of surprise and that He often answers her prayers in ways that surpass and transcend her own dreams and desires.

Every ballet dancer must overcome challenges, including injuries, long hours of practice, and the pain of tired muscles. Similarly, women with hearts that dance with the Lord must overcome challenges. Prolonged trials are the most difficult. Surely you have had to repeatedly deal with something that seemed to go on and on. Regardless of how much you pray, whom you run to for help, and how much money you spend to resolve the difficulty, still it continues. In fact, sometimes your trial worsens, evolving into an impossible situation and the dark night of the soul. You may even find yourself on the edge of despair and hopelessness.

The New Testament records the story of one woman who knew the debilitating experience of a prolonged trial. She suffered from out-of-control bleeding, a hemorrhagic condition continuing day after day, year after year, for 12 years. *When will this terrible night end?* she may have wondered. During days of bleeding, a woman was rendered unclean and could not be touched, according to Leviticus 15:25-27. This precious woman became an outcast—not just for days, but for years. Her mind calculated her resources and possibilities. In the beginning, she may have thought, *I'll just go to the physician, and he will know what to do.* She paid the price for help, and yet the prescribed treatment did not change her condition.

Someone may have suggested, "How about trying another physician? This one should be able to help you." She tried again, but still her condition did not get any better. She spent more and more money, trying every new treatment available, but her condition got worse with each passing year. She soon began to face the fact that she had an incurable disease.

Her suffering included its own set of unpalatable circumstances. No one wanted to come near her, for to touch her rendered one unclean. So she was rejected, avoided, untouchable. Her condition forced her into a new identity: She was an outcast. And to make matters worse, she spent every penny she had trying to get better. Now she was without any kind of financial resource. Perhaps the most difficult part of her trial was living with the fact that she was incurable—her condition worsened each year. She couldn't get better regardless of how much she tried. Her trial became not only agonizingly prolonged but also seemingly impossible.

But she must have heard the news about Jesus. "Have you heard about this teacher? People with diseases and incurable conditions like paralysis are coming to Him. And He is able to do what no normal man can do—He heals these afflicted men and women! The blind can see, the deaf can hear, and the lame can walk. Maybe He could heal you!"

At first, she might not have wanted to get her hopes up. After all, she had tried many therapies and been disappointed every time. But then she might have thought about the eyewitness accounts of Jesus' miracles. She must have begun to entertain the possibility that she could receive a miracle too. The more she thought about Jesus, the more hope filled her heart and soul. Soon her yearning thoughts for a way out of her pain turned to action. *I must see Jesus.*

A large crowd gathered around Jesus by the seashore. The suffering woman approached warily, but when she saw the crowd, she hesitated. After all, she was not accustomed to the presence of so many people.

Just when she began to let herself believe that Jesus might be willing and able to heal her, someone much more important caught Jesus' attention. Jairus, a synagogue official, pushed through the crowd, fell at Jesus' feet, and implored Him earnestly, "My little daughter is at the point of death; please come and lay Your hands on her, so that she will get well and live" (Mark 5:23). Jesus turned to walk with Jairus to his home. The large crowd moved with Him, and many pressed in on Him. The crowd was so imposing, and now Jesus was leaving with such an important person...perhaps the woman began to lose hope.

But no, it was now or never. She stepped beyond any fears or doubts that may have been crowding her mind, and she stepped out in faith. Ever more desperate to touch Jesus and be healed, she knew in her heart if she could just get close to Him, she would no longer live with the pain of her affliction. She thought, "If I just touch His garments, I will get well" (verse 28). She followed along and, little by little, made her way through the clamoring crowd of men and women, gradually moving closer and closer to Jesus. Finally, seeing a narrow opening between two people and catching just a glimpse of His robe, she reached out her hand and touched it.

Immediately, with just that simple touch, a new sensation filled her body! The flow of blood stopped, and she knew—she could feel it!—she was healed of her affliction. Now, wishing only to escape unnoticed, she tried to disappear into the crowd.

Jesus instantly knew that someone had received a powerful touch from Him, and He immediately turned around and asked, "Who touched my garments?" Trembling with fear, the woman's heart sank. The startled crowd grew quiet, and Jesus' disciples gently pointed out that many had been pressing in on Him. Was this her chance to get away? Might she be able to escape unnoticed? But Jesus persisted, telling everyone that someone did indeed touch Him and that power had gone out of Him (Luke 8:46).

As Jesus looked out over the hushed onlookers, she saw His face and suddenly knew what she must do. Trembling, she eased through the crowd and fell down before Him. Would He be offended by her presumptuous actions? Would He denounce her, an unclean woman, for touching Him? In a confused jumble of fear and gratitude, anxiety and relief, her confession poured out, flowing from her heart: "I didn't mean…I thought if I could just touch You…I just wanted to be healed, and I knew that You…Thank You so much…I'm so sorry if…" What would He say? What would He do?

But oh, how Jesus loved her! Oh, how His heart ached for all she had suffered, for the confusion that remained in her heart! Didn't she realize that He was not accusing her, that He was inviting her to know what just happened, inviting her to know Him? She was still thinking like an outcast, but Jesus loved her bold determination. She was willing to slip away unnoticed, but He was ready to dance!

If this were a movie, I imagine the crowd disappearing from the picture completely, and only two remain—Jesus and this precious woman. His focus was only on her, for He was ready to extend His surprising invitation: "Daughter, your faith has made you well; go in peace and be healed of your affliction" (Mark 5:34).

Wait…what did He say? She could hardly believe the first word out of His mouth! What did he call her—*daughter*? That word must have been music to her ears. She was no longer an outcast; Jesus called her *daughter*! She was not unclean any longer; Jesus healed her! And rather than condemning her actions, He commended her faith. Rather than banishing her, He blessed her with peace. And by encouraging her to go, He sent her into a brand-new life. He healed her through and through, outwardly and inwardly.

This woman is nameless in the Bible, and that's a good thing. We are all this woman, in our dark nights of the soul, bleeding even in our very hearts over impossible situations that have no easy remedies or good answers. Living on the edge of hope or despair, we hear about Jesus. And we reach out to Him in prayer, crying out to Him, leaning into His embrace, and touching the hem of His garment by faith, knowing He will somehow surprise us in our impossible situations. When we step out in faith like the woman in the story, we start by forsaking all else to trust Him. Eventually we don't even look back anymore as we forget what is behind us and run toward the fantastic adventure of trusting Him.

This blessed woman teaches that to have a woman's heart that dances, we can't play it safe any longer. Instead, we press through, lean in, and touch the hem of His garment with a radical faith and a reckless abandonment to His will. And when we do, we are often surprised to discover the new ways Jesus wants to dance with us.

I have a secret collection of thousands of surprises I've received from the Lord. Each one is wonderful, but I have some favorites. I'm sure you have your own surprises from Him too. I think heaven will be a marvelous place where perhaps we can sit together and share the surprises of the Lord.

About a year ago I spoke at a conference in Dallas. One woman named Nell had traveled from Selma, Alabama, and when I met her, she said to me, "Catherine, I wish you could meet my Bible study teacher. You would *love* her." I smiled at the way she emphasized the word *love*.

"Nell, I wish I could meet her too."

"Let me show you her Bible study notes," Nell said. "I brought them for you to see."

I looked at the handwritten notes of a 90-year-old Bible study teacher named Clara and gasped in awe. "Nell, these are amazing— so detailed and complete!"

"I tell you, Catherine, she's the best Bible study teacher. We love her! She copies these notes for us every week."

Sometime later, I had the opportunity to travel to Selma, Alabama, to speak at a weekend revival conference. Guess who I got to meet!

Clara! The first night of the conference, Nell came up to me and said, "Catherine, this is Clara!"

I hugged Clara and said, "Oh Clara, I'm so thrilled to meet you." The next morning when I arrived, Clara was waiting for me. "Catherine, come sit down with me for a minute. I want to talk with you."

A bit of fear struck my heart. *Oh, no—I hope I didn't say something that offended someone.* With a little uncertainty, I said, "Okay, Clara."

Then Clara began telling me her story. "Many years ago, back during the Depression, my husband (who is now with the Lord) told me he wanted to get me a gift. He asked me, 'What would you like for a gift, Clara?' I told him, 'I would love to have a cross for a necklace.' So he gave me a simple cross.

"Now Catherine, I wanted to give you something special, a treasure, something that was important to me. So I want you to have this." She pulled out a little yellow box and handed it to me.

Excitedly, I opened it and saw a beautiful, simple gold cross. As my tears began to flow, I said, "Clara, you can't give me this."

But she was not to be denied. "Catherine, I love you. I want you to have it and wear it."

What a surprise from the Lord! Never in a million years did I expect to have something so precious and meaningful as that gold cross. I wear it now as a remembrance of Clara and her devotion and commitment to the Lord. And when I look at the gold cross, I think of the special surprise gifts from the Lord that remind me of His love and His sacrifice on the cross for me.

Another unexpected surprise from God occurred during a time of discouragement. I was sitting in my office at Southwest Community Church, mulling over some unrealized dreams. Have you ever just mulled over the circumstances of your life? I seem to have a gift for mulling. And finally, I just have to let it go and trust God with whatever is bothering me. I prayed, *Lord, I wish these certain things would*

happen. But I trust in You and in Your plan. I do. But God, what are
You doing? I mean, what is happening?

In less than five minutes, my cell phone rang. It was Kayla, my
assistant at Quiet Time Ministries. "Cath, do you remember that order
from South Korea a few months ago?"

"Yes," I responded, intrigued by the tone in her voice.

"Well, you're not going to believe this. I just received a call from
three South Korean pastors, and they would like to meet you."

"Great—let's set up a meeting," I said.

Kayla responded with more urgency, "You don't understand. They're
driving here from Los Angeles, and they'll be here at the training
center in fifteen minutes!"

I was overwhelmed. "Are you kidding?"

"No," she responded, "I'm serious. They'll be here in fifteen minutes."

Well, as surprised as I was, I was also very touched and very hum-
bled. Who would drive three hours without an appointment, hoping
they could meet me? I felt so unworthy to have such a blessing heaped
on me. I said, "I'll be right there."

When I walked in to our training center offices, the three pastors
had already arrived, and Kayla was showing them our facility. One
pastor walked up to me, smiled, and introduced himself.

"I'm so glad to meet you," he said. He explained that he led a Korean
church on the Southern California coast. Then he introduced me to
the other two pastors.

One of the pastors said, "Catherine, I'm the director of a large religious organization in South Korea. I work with many of the pastors
there. We have 200,000 men and women who faithfully spend quiet
time with the Lord in the Bible every day. But now these people are
telling us that they want to know God more and grow deeper in their
relationship with Him. We believe your books and quiet times materials are the answer to help them grow more. We've already arranged
to have two of your books translated into Korean."

I was deeply touched with what these dear brothers in the Lord were sharing with me. I was also overwhelmed—I doubt my eyes have ever gotten so big.

Then they asked, "Would you be willing to talk with us about what we can share with our people in South Korea?"

"Right here?" I asked. "Right now?"

"Yes, could you?" They repeated, smiling and nodding with affirmation.

Such a request was a blessing to my heart. Oh, if only believers all across our world carried such hunger and thirst in their heart to grow in their faith in Christ. I think we would see an amazing revival sweep the world. I began sharing, in shortened version, all the main principles I teach about quiet time and Bible study. I said, "Whenever I teach on quiet time, I start with the basics—the importance of having a time, a place, and a plan." These pastors wrote down everything I said.

I continued, "The plan I love to teach in quiet time is according to the acronym, PRAYER:

Prepare Your Heart

Read and Study God's Word

Adore God in Prayer

Yield Yourself to God

Enjoy His Presence

Rest in His Love

I watched as these pastors were taking notes, thinking, *Who am I? What in the world is God doing here?* And that was exactly the surprise of God to me. I realized in a new way what He was doing *in the world*! For the next hour, we talked together about quiet time and devotional Bible study.

Then one of the pastors looked at me and said, "Could we pray together?"

"I would love to," I replied. Then the two from South Korea looked and asked me a question I could not understand. I looked at the man who spoke English and asked, "What do they want?"

"They would like to know if it's okay with you if they speak in Korean when they pray." With tears glistening in my eyes, I smiled and nodded my head. Then they all held out their hands, and together, holding hands, we prayed for God to work in a miraculous way in the lives of men and women in South Korea and throughout the world. We sent them on their way with tearful goodbyes and a lot of books. God's surprise that day was life-changing for me. I learned not to question the work of God and instead to trust Him to accomplish His plan, His way, in His time.

Many years ago, I heard Ney Bailey share at a Campus Crusade conference, "You be responsible for the depth of your ministry and let God be responsible for the breadth of your ministry." Oh how true those words have been for me. I have learned again and again to focus on my dance with the Lord and trust Him to tell the story in His own way and in His own time.

God has surprised me in many different ways. But without a doubt, one surprise stands out above all others in my dance. It came on a day I'll never forget—a moment when God seemed to reach out of the sky with a present wrapped especially for me. I never knew it would happen, but it did: God gave me back my dad.

My dad was like a knight in shining armor to me. I loved him with all my heart because he was my dad. When he came to visit my brother and me on rare occasions in our childhood, life was more exciting. I just loved being with him. But we hardly spent any time together.

One very special day changed everything in my relationship with my father. The day David asked me to marry him, I called my dad and said, "Dad, I'm engaged. I'm getting married."

He said with excitement, "Well, I would like to meet David. How about I fly in, and we'll meet for dinner?"

I replied, "Dad, I would love that!" To think about this even now overwhelms me.

When the day arrived, I was nervous. I can't even explain my feelings. Having this opportunity to introduce the man of my dreams to my dad was deeply meaningful for me. I was not used to sharing something so important with my dad. Walking up to the front door of that restaurant with David, my heart was racing. But David, always the confident one, was not a bit daunted.

We walked in the restaurant together, and there was my dad. He walked up with a big smile, extended his hand, and said, "You must be David." After they shook hands, Dad turned to me and smiled and hugged me. "Congratulations, honey. I'm so happy for you." In that welcome, all the years seemed to roll away, and I was my father's daughter. For the next two hours, we laughed, ate, and had the best time together.

When I walked down the aisle for my wedding, I looked into my dad's handsome face and saw tears in his eyes. But that's not all I saw in his eyes. I also saw his love for me and a great pride for both my new husband and me. And in that moment I realized something new, life-changing, and profound about my relationship with my father. I had thought about the circumstances of my relationship with my father only from my point of view. Now I realized that not only had I lost a relationship with my dad early on, but my dad had also lost a relationship with his daughter for all those years.

Well, my dad and I quickly made up for lost time. He began visiting David and me frequently. We spent many hours talking and laughing and getting to know one another. Guess what I discovered? I am not only a lot like my mother but also very much like my dad. In fact, knowing my dad—his thoughts, his hopes, his dreams, his personality, his joys, and his sorrows—has helped me know and understand myself better. What a surprise God gave me when I got married. I never expected such blessing, but I'm convinced God knew He was going to give me back my dad. What a wedding present from my Lord!

During the days after my mother's neck injury, when we didn't know if she would live or die, my father became a great strength for me. He stood with me through our entire ordeal. One afternoon, we sat on the floor, watching television and talking. He said, "Cath, what a life I've had."

"Tell me about it, Dad." And for the next three hours he told me all about his life, from the time he first married Mother to the present. Sharing his life experiences that day brought me so much closer and made me feel as though I had not missed any time at all with my father.

Now my dad and I are best friends. We talk on the phone all the time. I tell him everything. To think about that first meeting with my husband at the restaurant makes me shake my head—it seems like a thousand years ago. Only the Lord could have designed such a surprise for me. But that's what He does when we dance. What a fantastic adventure we experience when we trust Him!

I wonder what surprises are awaiting you in your dance with the Lord. Your eternal dance Partner is the God who loves to surprise you when you least expect it. So get ready, lean in, and watch for what He will do.

When I received the book of ballerina paintings from my gifted friend Kathleen Rousar, I remember thinking to myself, *She has captured in these paintings what was in my heart when I began to think and write about the dance.* I wrote to Kathleen, expressing my sheer delight in her gift to me. The more I looked at Kathleen's artwork, the more I dreamed about combining her paintings with my writing about a woman's heart that dances. I prayed, *Lord, I would love for her paintings to be seen by people throughout the world.* And then God surprised me again, opening the door for this book and for Kathleen's paintings to be included on the cover and in the interior.

I love Kathleen's explanation to me about why she originally painted her ballerinas in black and white with pink shoes. "When you dance with Jesus, He moves your life from simple black and white to full living color." Just look at the cover of this book, and you will see a woman whose heart dances with the Lord. Her arms and hands extend with gracefulness and beauty, qualities that flow from a heart touched by the Holy Spirit. Adorned with a beautiful flowing dress, she is perfectly attired to dance with her Prince, the Lover of her soul. Her shoes are the finest, one toe pointing forward, awaiting her dance. And now, she is looking upward and away, for her eyes are on her eternal Partner, saying, *Yes, Lord, I will dance with You*. She is eagerly waiting and watching, ready for the steps and surprises of the dance. May you and I be that woman with a heart ready to dance with her Lord.

12

Forever

"C atherine, you look beautiful," my bridesmaids Andy and Dottie said, admiring me in the dress I had dreamed of since I was a little girl—my wedding dress. I gazed at my image in the massive floor-to-ceiling mirror. I saw myself a bride, engaged, and soon to be married to the love of my life, David. I knew that I would know *the* dress when I saw it, and without a doubt, this was it. It had everything I wanted—lace, a satin skirt covered with filmy netting, and a long satin train. The train was something I had always imagined following me when I walked down the aisle. And then I put the veil on, the length of it flowing behind me beyond the edge of my dress. Looking again in the mirror, I put the finishing touches on my makeup and took a deep breath, knowing that the next time I looked in the mirror, the reflection would be that of a married woman. I could hardly believe it. I was getting married—something I never thought would happen to me. My soon-to-be husband was everything I had hoped for and so much more.

"Catherine, it's time." My brother grabbed my arm and proudly led me into the main chapel. The organist began the "Bridal Chorus," and everyone stood. The white runner had been rolled down the center aisle where I would walk—a tradition that I had witnessed many times as a little girl when I sat beside my mother as she played the organ for weddings. I definitely wanted that white runner for my own wedding. I had dreamed of my wedding my whole life. Sometimes I would lie in bed and imagine walking down the aisle of the church in my wedding dress.

I'm really getting married. I'm the bride. I can't believe it, I thought. I began the walk to the altar at the front of the little country church in Julian, California. *There he is!* I looked into my David's face from afar. *I'm going to be married to him—the fulfillment of one of my greatest dreams. Something I never believed would happen. I'm getting married!*

Smiling, David looked adoringly in my direction, waiting for me. *I feel like I've known this man all my life.* That's really how I felt. I reached the bottom of the stairs leading to the altar. I looked down at the floor to begin the walk up the steps to my beloved. But then my eyes widened. *Oh no...* The white runner had somehow become irregularly stretched over the stairs, and I couldn't actually see the first step.

"Catherine, grab my arm," David whispered, reaching down to me from above. I immediately grabbed his outstretched hand and leaned on his strength as he helped me walk up what were, to me, invisible stairs. He was my rescuer in that moment, anticipating my trouble.

We stood together, facing Josh McDowell, who conducted our wedding ceremony. Josh smiled, beginning his words with our names, "Cath and David..." Before I knew it, 15 minutes had passed, and he had finished by joking, "You will discover that marriage doubles your pleasures and triples your expenses." We all laughed together. It was a golden, stellar, memorable day—one I will never forget.

My husband and I just celebrated our twenty-seventh anniversary with a special dinner together. "Can you believe we've been married these many years?" we both remarked. I look into his face, so precious to me now. And though I see more lines now than I saw the day we married, he is more handsome to me today than ever before. My friend Dottie was right—the waters do run deeper with time.

I wonder if that feeling of deep love that results from time and experience together is just a taste of what I'll feel when I see the face of my Lord and step into His forever embrace in heaven. A life with God is waiting for us in heaven and will surpass anything we have experienced with Him here on earth.

Imagine the greatest time you have had on earth. Then multiply it by infinity, and still you haven't even scratched the very surface of heaven. Paul refers to "things which eye has not seen and ear has not heard, and which have not entered the heart of man, all that God has prepared for those who love Him" (1 Corinthians 2:9-10). As exciting as marriage on earth may be, we have another wedding to anticipate, and a marriage much more permanent and eternal.

After my earthly wedding day so many years ago, I experienced a new realization—all that I had dreamed of for my wedding was over in less than a day. I had spent hours dreaming about something that lasted only 24 hours—a wedding that included wearing the wedding dress and veil of my dreams, and walking down the aisle just as I had imagined.

Someday we are going to be presented to our eternal Bridegroom, Jesus, as His bride in a heavenly wedding with a wedding feast called the marriage supper of the Lamb (Revelation 19:9). The bride of Jesus Christ will shine with the glory of God (Revelation 21:11), and you will bear His name on your forehead, displaying for all to see that you belong to Him (Revelation 22:4). When you meet the One who has been and is your eternal dance Partner, you will be ready and adorned for Him (Revelation 21:2).

Your great joy will be His personal touch when He wipes every tear from your eyes, takes away every sadness, stops all crying, and eliminates every pain from your experience (Revelation 21:4). This singular promise is perhaps one of the most precious of all we look forward to in heaven.

My friend Skip just recently stepped into the face-to-face, forever embrace of his Lord. He suffered the pain of a devastating cancer that consumed his body. Our church family loved him and prayed with him through his journey of pain and suffering. I received the news in an e-mail that he is now "present with the Lord." Tears came from deep in my heart. But the news was bittersweet, for now I know he has no pain.

Heaven will be a new experience for us, with no more sadness or pain. My mother will dance in a way she cannot now, for she will no longer be sitting in a wheelchair. There is no multiple sclerosis in heaven. I won't need the medication I rely on now for migraine headaches, for there are no headaches in heaven—praise the Lord! Charles Spurgeon will never be bedridden or laid low, for there is no gout or depression in heaven. Joni Eareckson won't need her wheelchair, for there is no paralysis in heaven. Heaven is going to be the greatest dance of all, with the Lord leading us all in moves we haven't begun to see here on earth.

My favorite ballerina painting by Kathleen Rousar is the one shown at the beginning of part 4 in this book. This dancer is different from all the others, for she is bowing low in worship, clearly in the presence of the King. Her heart of worship, love, and devotion radiates through her face. Her flowing dress with its many folds touches the ground. And this ballerina has her hand touching her shoe, as if to say, "Lord, I am ready to dance with You. I can't wait to look into Your face."

Heaven will include a new relationship with our dance Partner, for we will see His face. To look into eyes I've only pictured in my imagination is going to be, for me, the greatest reward of all. Amy Carmichael says, "No strange face will meet us on that Day, we shall be awakened by the vision of His face."[1] I can look forward to seeing the face of "the God who has led me all my life long" (Genesis 48:15 RSV).

One of the greatest complexities of my life is dancing in the here and now in anticipation of eternity. We are assured of the eternal embrace, and that is our blessed hope. We can never lose His love or His forgiveness. We know His grace. Our dance with the Lord is one filled with hope, and our Lord continually builds our hope with each new promise He gives us from His Word as we dance with Him. Seeing the face of my Lord someday is the great hope I live for. I am going to look into His eyes.

～ ⁕ ～

She stood at a distance, one in a crowd of many, looking with shock and horror at the spectacle of the crucifixion. This was no ordinary crucifixion, for Mary Magdalene knew the One on this cross. *Why doesn't He save Himself? Please, Jesus, command the armies of heaven to come and rescue You!* she may have thought. For she knew He was the Lord, the Christ, the Messiah. And He could work miracles. She had watched Him heal paralyzed bodies, blind eyes, deaf ears, and mute tongues. She had seen Him feed more than five thousand people with only five loaves of bread and two fish.

But more than that, she had experienced His power in her own body. Over the years she had lost herself to a power that had taken control of her body, her mind, and her thoughts. Hollow-eyed and desperate, she had given up all hope of a life. No one could even come near her because of the darkness that had pervaded her being. But one person was not put off. In fact, He found her, not the other way around. Even though a force inside of her seemed to keep her from this One, He was greater and more powerful.

Jesus found her, like a lost sheep, and welcomed her with love. He immediately knew her suffering and the cause of it. More accurately, the *causes* (plural)—seven demons had taken control of every part of her being. In an instant, He commanded those seven demons to leave her. The demons had no choice, for His authority was certain and absolute over them. They left her body, and she became Mary Magdalene once again. *I'm free!* she thought, wanting to shout to everyone in her town. But she didn't need to say anything, for everyone who saw her instantly knew she had been changed. Her dramatic transformation was clear for all to see.

And now the One she had followed and learned from during His public ministry was near death. Seeing His agony, she longed to comfort Him. But she did not dare—not with the Roman soldiers positioned around Him. The danger was palpable. Suspicion abounded, and anything could happen. This crucifixion was the Romans' show and the religious leaders' also—they were controlling everything about it.

Mary Magdalene stood with other women who had become as close as sisters to her—Mary the mother of James the Less and Joseph, Salome, and the mother of James and John. Some of them had left their normal responsibilities and traveled together so they could minister to Jesus and the disciples, making sure they had food and accommodations. They all made quite a band of travelers—Jesus, the 12 disciples, and the ministering women. Mary considered the travel a privilege, for she loved to hear Jesus teach.

Now she was spent with sorrow and weeping, and helplessness began to set in. *There is nothing I can do. Nothing I can do to save Him. Nothing I can do to minister to Him. He did everything for me, and I can do nothing.* All the disciples had fled except for John, who was standing with Jesus' mother. Everyone was seemingly paralyzed, feet glued to the ground, watching only One—Jesus. Mary heard very little from Him and knew that the excruciating end to His crucifixion— suffocation—was coming soon. Blood was everywhere, and His brutalized body on the cross was a gruesome sight. As His life was ending, so were all her hopes and joys in life.

Just at that moment, while she was looking toward the cross, she heard her Master cry out three words. Unusual and unexpected words— "It is finished." And then He breathed His last. Sorrow and grief overcame this small band of women who had stayed until the very end.

Mary watched Joseph of Arimathea, a member of the Sanhedrin, and Nicodemus, another ruler of the Jews, take Jesus' body from the cross. Racing time as the Sabbath approached, Joseph and Nicodemus quickly bound the body with strips of linen and spices according to the custom of the Jews for burial (John 19:40). Mary Magdalene and Mary the mother of Joses secretly followed Joseph and Nicodemus, watching as they laid Jesus' body in a tomb. Jesus deserved a more proper preparation and burial, and the two women were determined to attend to His burial themselves. Returning home, they prepared spices and perfumes and then rested on the Sabbath as the law required. Mary Magdalene set her mind on only one thing—being near Jesus.

The sun was only beginning to peek through the leaves and branches of the trees early Sunday morning as Mary Magdalene, Salome, and Mary the mother of Joses ran back to the tomb. As they neared, they felt as though they had just been here. But what was this? Alarmed, they ran toward the tomb. It was clearly not as Mary had seen it prior to the Sabbath. The stone covering the opening to the tomb was rolled to the side, but it was far too heavy for one person to move. What was going on? And where were the Roman soldiers who were supposed to be making sure no one disturbed the tomb or took the body? Leaning in, their worst fears were realized. The body was gone! Someone had stolen the body of Jesus! What were they to do?

While they were trying to come to grips with the mystery of Jesus' missing body, brightness suddenly filled the tomb. Two men instantly appeared in dazzling clothing. The women, overpowered by the shining of their appearance, fell facedown on the ground, terrified. But the men's message was the best news this world has ever heard: Jesus is alive! "Why do you seek the living One among the dead? He is not here, but He has risen" (Luke 24:5-6). Running back to the disciples, they reported what they had seen. "The body is gone! Two men who looked like angels told us Jesus is alive again!"

Just think—these women were the very first to hear the good news that would be proclaimed not only to the 12 disciples but also to the world down through the centuries and to this very day. Of course, not everyone believes at first in our day, and such was the case then. Even the disciples didn't respond well to the news at first. "Impossible. Nonsense. This can't be!"

But they needed to be sure. Peter and John ran to the tomb to see if what the women had said was true. First John arrived at the tomb. Looking in, he saw only the linen wrappings lying there. Peter caught up to John and actually entered the tomb. The face cloth was rolled up, and the body was gone! John also entered the tomb and saw for himself. Jesus was not there.

Mary Magdalene had followed them back to the tomb but could not run as fast. She arrived just as they were leaving to go back home. Losing Jesus was bad enough, but must they lose His body too? The sorrow hit her heart with full force. She stood outside the tomb, overcome with grief and weeping uncontrollably. She couldn't even give Jesus' body a proper burial, for it was gone.

Devastated, she looked into the tomb one more time. She gasped! Two angels were sitting where the body had been—one where Jesus' head had been and one where His feet had been—as if to punctuate the fact that His body was simply not there. Before she had time to entertain another thought, they said, "Woman, why are you weeping?" Perhaps they said those words incredulously, for they knew the truth—Jesus had indeed risen from the dead.

But Mary was not yet sure. She was emotionally broken from the trauma of watching her Master die. She had faithfully followed this One who had given her, a woman in bondage to demons, a new freedom, unconditional love, and undeserved respect. And now He was gone. Brokenhearted, she said to the angels, "Because they have taken away my Lord, and I do not know where they have laid Him" (John 20:13).

Just as she said those words, she sensed a new presence. Someone else was near. She turned around and saw the figure of a man framed by light coming from the open tomb. Who is this? The gardener, perhaps? Who else would be near this tomb so early in the morning? The man asked her the same question the angels had asked: "Woman, why are you weeping? Whom are you seeking?"

Yes, Mary was indeed seeking, just as this mysterious person had said. But her broken heart could not perceive the promise or the invitation to dance implied in this man's question. She didn't realize He was the One who had promised that those who seek will ultimately find. She didn't connect his words with the promise of Jeremiah the prophet:

"You will seek Me and find Me when you search for Me with all your heart" (Jeremiah 29:13). Lost in the fog of her grief and shock at the loss of Jesus, she said to this man, "Sir, if you have carried Him away, tell me where you have laid Him, and I will take Him away." This new thought seemed more logical—perhaps this man, probably a gardener, had taken the body. Loyal until the end to follow Jesus and faithful to serve Him, she desired to ensure His protection at least in death. She would watch over the body herself if she could just find it.

"Mary!"

His voice! That was enough for her. She finally recognized her beloved Teacher, for no one spoke her name the way He did. "Rabboni!" she said, falling before Him and holding on to Him, determined to never let Him go again. Jesus gave His blessed disciple Mary the honor of appearing to her first before anyone else. He could have appeared to Peter or John, but no, He chose Mary Magdalene, a woman who had been demon-possessed but set free—free to follow and love and serve her Lord, free to dance with Him.

Jesus then gave Mary a new assignment, her first real ministry of service following the resurrection. "Go to My brethren and say to them, 'I ascend to My Father and your Father, and My God and your God'" (John 20:17). She became His messenger, sharing the good news of His resurrection and also His impending ascension to the Father.

"I have seen the Lord!" She breathlessly told the other disciples His words about the ascension. The news was both happy and sad, at least for the disciples at that moment. He was alive! He had returned! But now He was going away again? Little did they know that although He would be going away, He would soon live with them in a whole new way, dwelling in them, working with them, empowering them, and doing great and mighty works in them—and through them, in the whole world—by the power of the Holy Spirit.

Oh, what a moment it must have been when Mary realized she was standing face-to-face with the risen Jesus! Hours of grief and sadness were wiped away in an instant when she saw His face and looked into His eyes. Oh, how they danced in that moment! That intimate time of devotion foreshadowed what was to come—she would follow His lead forever into eternity. And lead He would. In fact, her first step in the dance was declaring the good news. She would set the example for all the others. When she arrived and shared her words with those disciples, she displayed her dance with Jesus for all to see. And they did not doubt—she had seen His face and heard Him call her name.

Oh, what glory the dance with Jesus brings! When you dance, you hear Him speak your name, for He knows your name (Isaiah 43:1). And when He leads, your steps with Him are on display for everyone in the world to see. When you dance, the world will be drawn to Jesus. With your eyes firmly fixed on eternity, as others have said,

> your mess becomes His message,
>
> your tests become His testimony,
>
> and your history becomes His story.

Just as the sun makes its majestic rise each morning, declaring the existence and majesty of God, so your dance with Jesus declares the glory of God to those who are watching.

Anne R. Cousin wrote the hymn *The Sands of Time Are Sinking*, expressing in her words the glory of stepping from time into eternity and seeing the face of our Bridegroom, the Lord Jesus. She begins with these words:

> The sands of time are sinking, the dawn of heaven breaks;
> The summer morn I've sighed for—the fair, sweet morn awakes;
> Dark, dark hath been the midnight, but dayspring is at hand,
> And glory—glory dwelleth in Immanuel's land.

> O Christ, He is the fountain, the deep, sweet well of love!
> The streams on earth I've tasted, more deep I'll drink above;

There, to an ocean fullness, His mercy doth expand,
And glory—glory dwelleth in Immanuel's land.

The King there in His beauty, without a veil is seen:
It were a well-spent journey, though seven deaths lay between.
The Lamb, with His fair army, doth on Mount Zion stand,
And glory—glory dwelleth in Immanuel's land.

My friend Julie tells the story of her mother, who loved this hymn and sang it often. She especially loved a stanza that begins, "The bride eyes not her garment, but her dear Bridegroom's face." Her mother was coming to the end of her journey here on earth following a diagnosis of cancer. She had fought valiantly, but now the pain was great, and she was about to step from time into eternity. Julie describes her last time together with her mother in the hospital.

> The family gathered, and we had a wonderful time of prayer around her bed one evening. She prayed for each of us. My dad and I took turns spending the night with her at the hospital. During the night I was "on duty," and she became rather restless and was talking—sometimes making sense and sometimes not. She wanted to get out of bed, so the nurse and I helped her. But as I got her back into bed, she looked at me and said, "Julie, get my brush, brush my hair...my bridegroom is coming!" I answered her through my tears, "Yes, mom, He sure is coming soon!" That was really my last interaction with her...and I would not have missed that last little interaction with her for anything! It has been such a comfort to me knowing that she is seeing her bridegroom face-to-face now and gazing on her king of grace!

I've wrestled on toward heaven, against storm and wind and
    tide,
Now, like a weary traveler that leaneth on his guide,
Amid the shades of evening, while sinks life's lingering sand,
I hail the glory dawning from Immanuel's land.

Oh! I am my Beloved's, and my Beloved's mine!
He brings a poor vile sinner into His "house of wine."
I stand upon His merit; I know no other stand,
Not even where glory dwelleth in Immanuel's Land.

One day, as we dance with the Lord, we will no longer embrace Him by faith "through a glass darkly," but face-to-face forever in eternity. I think about seeing His face and looking into His eyes. Will my mind shuffle through myriads of experiences with Him? Or will I simply fall on my face before Him? I believe the moment will transcend time and any earthly event or experience. I know I will be marked with His name. And I don't think I'll be looking at myself but only at Him when He welcomes me home.

But this I know: We will dance. Jesus assured Philip, and He assures you and me, "I go to prepare a place for you...I will come again and receive you to Myself, that where I am, there you may be also" (John 14:2-3). There, my friend, is your sure promise of an eternal embrace with your Lord in the forever dance with Him. And when you see His face, you will become like Him, for you shall see Him as He is (1 John 3:2). You will see Immanuel, the Son of David, the Rose of Sharon, our Redeemer, Wonderful Counselor, and Prince of Peace, the King of kings and Lord of lords, our Master, Teacher, and Savior, the good shepherd, the bread of life, the Light of the world, the way, the truth, and the life, the true vine, the Lion of the tribe of Judah, the Lamb, and the bright morning star. And you will see so much more. Only eternity can tell the whole story of all He is, forever and ever and ever.

Those who dance with Him cultivate a view to eternity, a heart to see forever. Imagine looking out at the broad expanse of the ocean. Seeming to go on forever and ever, the water appears to meet the sky at the horizon. And yet what you see is not all there is. By faith, you know there is more. You just can't see it, for your view is limited. Those with hearts to see forever don't look at life or eternity from the vantage point of the here and now or feelings and emotions. No, they look instead from the firm ground of God and His Word and thus live in the eternal perspective—able to see all of life from God's point of view and live accordingly in the present. With the vantage point of the eternal clearly in view, they live with the knowledge that there is so much more that is theirs in eternity. As a result, they are filled with hope. They know and live with assurance that the eternal truth they see in the Word of God is indeed the true meaning of life.

Life for these people is all about their dance with the Lord. Therefore, they enter into the dance daily, moment by moment. Friend, as you continue on life's journey, you are going to be faced with obstacles and fiery trials that will occasionally tempt you to stop dancing. Don't stop. Lean in a little closer and watch how the Lord will lift you up and carry you in the dance.

May you join that great company of men and women whose hearts dance with the Lord. In light of your forever embrace with your eternal Partner, may you dance today, dear friend. Just dance.

> The Bride eyes not her garment, but her dear
> Bridegroom's face;
> I will not gaze at glory, but on my King of grace;
> Not at the crown He giveth, but on His pierced hand.
> The Lamb is all the glory of Immanuel's land.

Notes

Chapter 1—Dance

1. Fergus Macdonald, "Shine on Us Again", *Encounter with God*, October–December 2008, 68.
2. Mardy Grothe, *I Never Metaphor I Didn't Like* (New York: HarperCollinsPublishers, 2008), 10.
3. A.W. Tozer, editorial, *Alliance Weekly*, June 3, 1950.

Chapter 2—Overture

1. Henri Nouwen, *The Return of the Prodigal Son* (New York: Doubleday, 1992), 106.

Chapter 3—Yes

1. Ann Kiemel, *Yes* (Wheaton, IL: Tyndale House, 1978), 11-12. Used by permission.

Chapter 4—Partners

1. John MacArthur, *Twelve Extraordinary Women* (Nashville: Thomas Nelson, 2005), 149.
2. Leo Tolstoy, *War and Peace* (New York: Alfred Knopf, 2007), 239-40.
3. John Piper, *Seeing and Savoring Jesus Christ* (Wheaton, IL: Crossway Books, 2001), 9.

Chapter 5—Reflection

1. Mindy Aloff, *Dance Anecdotes* (New York: Oxford University Press, 2006), 1.
2. Aloff, *Dance Anecdotes*, 2.
3. Charles Spurgeon, *Morning and Evening* (Peabody, MA: Hendrickson, 2006). See the morning entry for February 1.
4. Max Lucado, *In the Grip of Grace* (Dallas: Word, 1996), 122-23.
5. Jennifer O'Neill, *From Fallen to Forgiven* (Nashville: W Publishing Group, 2001), 37.
6. O'Neill, *From Fallen to Forgiven*, 34.
7. Henri Nouwen, *Beloved* (Grand Rapids: Eerdmans, 2007), 19-20.
8. Used by permission of Conni Hudson, Journeying with Jesus (www.journeying withJesus.org) © 2001. All rights reserved.

Chapter 6—Devotion

1. Nancy Ellison, *The Ballet Book* (New York: Universe, 2003), 41.
2. Hannah Whitall Smith, *The Unselfishness of God* (New York: Revell, 1903), 193.
3. Andrew Murray, *With Christ in the School of Prayer* (New Kensington, PA: Whitaker House, 1981), 24.
4. For more information about quiet time and the PRAYER quiet time plan, see Catherine Martin, *Six Secrets to a Powerful Quiet Time* (Eugene, OR: Harvest House, 2006).
5. Kay Arthur, Jill Briscoe, and Carole Mayhall, *Can a Busy Christian Develop Her Spiritual Life?* (Minneapolis: Bethany House, 1994), 25.
6. Arthur, et al., *Can a Busy Christian Develop Her Spiritual Life?*, 31.
7. Lori Sakkab. Used by permission.

Chapter 7—Embrace

1. Nancy Leigh DeMoss, *Surrender* (Chicago: Moody, 2003), 55.
2. Kiemel, *Yes*, 10. Used by permission.

Chapter 8—Steps

1. Agrippina Vaganova, *Basic Principles of Classical Ballet* (New York: Dover, 1969), vi.
2. Max Lucado, *Traveling Light* (Nashville: W Publishing Group, 2001), 29.
3. John Piper, *A Hunger for God* (Wheaton, IL: Crossway, 1997), 23.
4. Ann Kiemel, *I Love the Word Impossible* (Wheaton, IL: Tyndale House, 1976), 119-20.
5. Carol Travilla and Joan Webb, *The Intentional Woman* (Colorado Springs: NavPress, 2002), 11.
6. Henri Nouwen, *Turn My Mourning into Dancing* (Nashville: Thomas Nelson, 2001), xv-xvi.
7. Author unknown.
8. Henry Morris, "Evidence of the Spirit's Filling," *Days of Praise,* December 2008–February 2009. See the entry for January 26, 2009.
9. Gladys Aylward and Christine Hunter, *The Little Women* (Chicago: Moody Press, 1999), 7-8.
10. Alan Burgess, *The Small Women* (Ann Arbor, MI: Servant Books, 1985), 149.

Chapter 9—Romance

1. Aloff, *Dance Anecdotes*, 32.
2. Aloff, *Dance Anecdotes*, 9.
3. Ellison, *The Ballet Book*, 24.
4. Henri Nouwen, *Heart Speaks to Heart* (Notre Dame: Ave Maria Press, 1989), 26-31.

Chapter 10—Story

1. Reprinted from the blog of Jeff Goins at jeffgoins.myadvertures.org. Used by permission.
2. George Watson, *Soul Food* (Cincinnati: Knapp, 1900), 81.

Chapter 12—Forever

1. Amy Carmichael, *Edges of His Ways* (Fort Washington, PA: Christian Literature Crusade, 1955), 9.

About the Author

Catherine Martin is a summa cum laude graduate of Bethel Theological Seminary with a master of arts degree in theological studies. She is founder and president of Quiet Time Ministries, director of women's ministries at Southwest Community Church in Indian Wells, California, and adjunct faculty member of Biola University. She is the author of many books and is senior editor for *Enriching Your Quiet Time* quarterly magazine. As a popular speaker at retreats and conferences, Catherine challenges others to seek God and love Him with all of their heart, soul, mind, and strength. For more information about Catherine, visit www.quiettime.org, www.catherinemartinonline.com, and www.cathsblog.com.

About Quiet Time Ministries

Quiet Time Ministries is a nonprofit organization offering resources for your quiet time. Visit us online at www.quiettime.org. The Quiet Time Ministries Resource and Training Center, located in Bermuda Dunes, California, offers conferences and workshops to encourage others in their relationship with the Lord.

Quiet Time Ministries
Post Office Box 14007
Palm Desert, CA 92255
1-800-925-6458
760-772-2357
www.quiettime.org

More Great Books by Catherine Martin
from Harvest House Publishers

Passionate Prayer

This intensely practical book encourages you to develop greater passion for God and for communion with Him. You will discover the power of talking with God, be reminded of His promises when you pray, and experience the privilege of an intimate prayer relationship.

    Companion volume: Passionate Prayer—A Quiet Time Experience

Trusting in the Names of God

Catherine presents the many names of God, describes how they reveal His character, and teaches that by trusting in them you can better understand who God is.

    Companion volume: Trusting in the Names of God—A Quiet Time Experience

Set My Heart on Fire

Thoroughly scriptural and theologically conservative, this passionate invitation to a life of obedience and holiness uses biblical teaching, inspirational stories, and personal anecdotes to gently but effectively lead you into a deeper walk with the Lord.

Walking with the God Who Cares

Catherine demonstrates how to experience a deep and abiding sense of joy in the midst of sorrow and pain: through an intimate relationship with the God who cares and a complete dependence on His Word. This 30–day journey is packed with inspiring stories, powerful promises, stimulating quiet time plans, and more.

Knowing and Loving the Bible

This powerful, interactive journey transforms reading and studying the Bible into acts of love and brings you closer to God as you discover nourishment for daily living and build a foundation on His promises.

Six Secrets to a Powerful Quiet Time

If you desire a close walk with God, a rich devotion time, and the joy of pursuing God, you will find inspiration, tools, and encouragement while exploring the *Six Secrets to a Powerful Quiet Time*.